SEVEN DAYS
IN THE
MISTS

A Memoir

NANCY M. BRITT

Flint Hills Publishing

Seven Days in the Mists A Memoir
© Nancy M. Britt 2024
All rights reserved.

Cover Design by Amy Albright

stonypointgraphics.weebly.com

Flint Hills Publishing
Topeka, Kansas
Tucson, Arizona
www.flinthillspublishing.com

Printed in the U.S.A.

This book reflects the author's present recollections of experiences over time and from her perspective. Some events and dialogue have been recreated.

Paperback Book: ISBN: 978-1-953583-77-2
Hardback Book ISBN: 978-1-953583-78-9
Electronic Book ISBN: 978-1-953583-79-6

.

Library of Congress Control Number Pending

DEDICATION

Dedicated in loving memory to my father, who taught me to not be afraid to wander.

Come away, O human child!
To the waters and the wild
With a faery, hand in hand,
For the world's more full of weeping
than you can understand.

W.B. Yeats, *The Stolen Child*

CONTENTS

PROLOGUE

Asleep, I've been
Blissful in slumber
Unaware of the seasons, of the changes

Millennia have passed before me
Empires have risen and fallen into dust

But I remain

My stones hold fast against the seas
My forests and grasses grow thick
The winds and rains cleanse me

In the void, I hear her

Tears of sorrow and desolation
She moans in the darkness
Confident none will hear

But I do

My child weeps
A sorrow she cannot express

But I know why

SEVEN DAYS IN THE MISTS

I come to her
In the night when she sleeps
I sweep back her hair and caress her cheek

I know what to do

I pull back the veil
slowly, the mists lift
And I call her home

TUCSON

Alone, I stood on the back patio and swirled the drink in my glass, listening to the ice clink against the sides. Light danced along the brick wall enclosing the backyard as the setting sun played upon the pool water. I wondered how many of us had ever wanted something, someone, so bad that we let it tear us apart. I did. And there wasn't a drink strong enough, a therapist wise enough, or a friend dear enough to put the pieces back together.

The starkness of the rocky, barren landscape of gravel and cacti that surrounded me contrasted with my memory of the soft earthen pathways through the forests and green woodlands of Ireland. I closed my eyes and reminisced.

Suddenly, my dog burst to life, running and barking and making her best attempt to appear ferocious.

"Fiadh," I called out. "Fiadh, stop it, stop it."

I half-heartedly tried to control her theatrics. I knew the door was open, and Jen would let herself in. For a moment, I stood frozen in indecision. How much should I reveal this evening?

Undaunted, my friend made her way into the house as Fiadh, my one-hundred-pound Cane Corso, danced for her attention. The chaos of her entrance did not end my trance, but if Jen noticed I was distracted, she neither cared nor tried to steal my attention.

"So, tell me about your trip. Did you have a good time?" Jen asked, pulling bottles of wine from her bag.

I shook my head to clear it and busied myself uncorking one of the bottles Jen had been eyeing. I handed her a glass, and we went to the patio to sit and enjoy the fall Sonoran evening. The monsoon season had ended and with it went the oppressive humidity. The sky was a riot of brilliant pinks and blues, slowly turning to red and purple as the sun descended on the western horizon. I smiled and sat down across from her.

"My trip was amazing," I said enthusiastically. "In fact, it's part of the reason I asked you over tonight. Okay, I lied. It's *the* reason I asked you over. I have so much to tell you."

"You mean you didn't just ask me over because you missed me?" Jen joked. "How callous of you."

We both laughed. Jen had no idea what was coming, and I still wasn't sure I was ready to reveal it.

"Let's see," I began. "The weather was mostly rainy; I spent large parts of every day lost; and most of my days ended up totally different than what I had planned. In other words, it was perfect."

"Enough of the pleasantries." Jen rolled her eyes. "I didn't come with bottles of wine to hear you drone on about the rainy weather in Ireland."

A pregnant pause ensued as I grappled with what I was about to ask of her. Jen was a former attorney who was now a mystery writer. She'd spent her whole career dissecting lies from the truth, and I could tell I wasn't about to get away with hiding in meaningless banter.

I looked at her and hesitantly said, "I think I want to write a book."

Jen was in the process of taking a sip of wine as I said this. She snorted out a laugh. "God, it was that great, huh? Who'd you shag?"

She lowered her glass, and her smile fell as she looked at me and realized I wasn't joking.

"Oh my God, you're serious," she said, mortified. "I'm so sorry. I thought you were messing with me."

I waved her off and laughed. "Don't worry about it. I totally understand. I'm the last person who thought I'd be saying that too. The fact is, I had an experience while I was there. Some might say it was life-altering. I guess only time will tell. But something happened to me, and now I feel a need to write about it."

I took a sip of my wine. Jen sat silently, watching me, giving me the space I needed to tell her why.

"It's crazy. I mean, who wants to read about my trip? But I think I'd like to try. Maybe it will help me make sense of it."

Jen got out of her chair, grabbed her glass of wine, and moved to the patio sofa. She placed the wineglass down on the end table and rearranged the pillows before climbing on. Then she leaned back and tucked her feet up. Once comfortable, she looked at me.

"Well, I guess you better tell me about Ireland."

I let out a sigh of relief. I looked at Jen and the stunning Santa Catalina Mountains with gratitude. The setting sun cast a rosy hue as shadows sculpted the rocky terrain. The contrast of light and dark brought out the depth of the mountains' canyons and stone-faced cliffs. *We are like the mountains. A monolithic mass at first, imposing, impenetrable, simplistic. But if we are lucky, the light shifts, the shadows play on us, and sometimes, someone sees our crevasses.*

The air was still, and the evening temperature pleasantly warm—a perfect night for storytelling. I remembered what I was thinking about just before she arrived, and I knew how I was to start this tale.

"To understand Ireland, I need to tell you first why I felt the need to go."

SANTA FE

I remember the sun beating down from a cloudless blue sky while I stared at the piñon-covered hill. As I listened to the ringtone of the number I had just called, my mind was in chaos. I had no idea what I was going to say. In the background, I listened to the loudspeakers call out the ring status for the various competition arenas. All around me was constant motion as horses and riders went back and forth between the competition rings and the stabling areas. Golf carts whizzed past, each overloaded with people, tack, and dogs. People shouted out to each other as they zipped by.

A voice came over the phone.

"Hi, this is Brynn. Please leave a message."

"Hey, Brynn," I answered. "Um…I…um, just checking in to let you know I'm in Santa Fe for one more day, and um…well, I hope we can get together for dinner and get caught up. Okay, well…um, hope all is well…um, talk to you soon."

As I hung up, I didn't hold out much hope that this would happen. I had come to Santa Fe for a two-week horse show, and this was the end of the second week. I called the first week, and she texted back that maybe we could get together the following week and include another mutual friend who was out of town until then.

Great, I'd thought, and then I didn't think any more of it. But now it was the end of my stay here, and I went back and forth on whether to reach out again. And, God's honest truth, I didn't blame her for not wanting to see me, given that the last time we met I was an hour late and drunk off my ass.

Sweat dripped off my nose as I thought about my unwavering ability to be a complete screw-up at times. Santa Fe seemed to bring out my demons. I had lived there for two years, and they were the

14

most challenging two years of my life. I came for love and left broken-hearted. Everything I did seemed to be wrong. My attempts to make friends were, at best, accepted with lukewarm interest. I had never experienced such isolation, before or since. With each passing day, I felt closer to madness.

When I finally decided to leave, I was broken. To say I have no love lost for the place would be an understatement. If it weren't for work, I wouldn't be in Santa Fe at all. Brynn and a few others were the only people I wished to remain connected to. Now it seemed I had just shortened that list, as it was clear she had no interest in remaining friends. Of course, that was the crux of the problem. I had never wanted to be just her friend.

And now I was almost done with a two-week stint in New Mexico, with one measly text exchange between Brynn and me to show for it. June, the owner of the barn I worked out of back in Tucson, was busy cleaning tack as our daily competitions had wrapped up.

"Still no word from your friend?" June asked.

"No," I replied curtly, afraid June would notice my disappointment.

June stopped what she was doing and looked over at me. My brusque tone was out of character. Self-conscious of my reaction, I grabbed a hose and started to fill water buckets.

"Well, maybe something came up. I'm sure you'll hear from her soon."

I weakly smiled. "Perhaps."

"Does that mean I get the pleasure of your company for dinner tonight?"

Despite my foul mood, I found myself laughing. "I guess so, such that it is."

"Perfect, her loss is my gain."

I chuckled to myself as I realized once again that she was my superhero. A diminutive woman in her seventies, barely over five feet tall and toothpick thin, I had never met a stronger person than her. We had just spent the last three months showing her young horses in California, Colorado, and finally here in New Mexico. Through it all she was right beside me, helping in whatever way she could.

I finished watering the horses and looked back at June working on cleaning the tack. I wondered if I would ever be able to adequately let her know how much her friendship meant to me and how her positive attitude had inspired me and helped me through the hard times these last three months. How much I appreciated that her faith in my abilities never wavered, even when I seriously doubted and second-guessed myself. Most importantly, how our end-of-the-day beer and talks were the best therapy sessions I had ever had.

While standing there, I thought about how hard last week had been. The heat had been brutal. One night after a tough day, I woke to a searing pain in the left side of my chest. Lying on my back, I felt like I was impaled on the bed. I could not move or speak, and as I lay there, I wondered if this was my end. It didn't seem fair; I had so much to do. I wasn't ready to check out.

Eventually, I rolled to my side and managed to reach the water glass. I took sips, and after about ten minutes, I felt the pain subside.

The following morning, I told June about my incident. Luckily, I was done competing with her horses for the week, so I could take it easy and recuperate. The incident shook me, but I wasn't willing to go to urgent care. I brushed it off as stress.

For the next few days, I lived like a monk, did my work early, got out of the heat, ate almost nothing but salad, and was back in my hotel room and in bed before eight. It seemed to work, and by the beginning of the next week, I felt much better and was able to continue competing.

Then disaster struck again. After a dinner of salad and chicken, I was rudely awakened by a gastrointestinal tsunami. I stumbled in the dark to the bathroom, and for the next twenty-four hours, this room was my home as I suffered through a horrible bout of food poisoning.

Now, at the end of our time in Santa Fe, I was exhausted and thankful this was our last show for the summer season. I longed to be back home, have a home-cooked meal, and sleep in my own bed. So, not hearing back from Brynn hadn't registered with me until now.

I felt empty and hollow as I finished the night chores of feeding and putting everything away. I really didn't have any excuses for feeling this way. My business was thriving and growing. I loved working with June and felt that I had finally found my home at her barn. The customers were fun, and everyone created a lovely community. But I couldn't hide the fact that I was upset that I hadn't heard from Brynn.

I grabbed a couple of beers from the cooler, opened them, and handed one to June. We each took a seat and stared out the now-empty competition rings. The sun had started its descent for the night, and the sky was transitioning from blue to purple.

In the silence between us, I found the space to feel my sorrow. And in that space, I found words.

"I loved her. Brynn. I guess I still do." I said, staring out at the hills, now just dark outlines against a purple sky. I looked over at June. "It didn't go as I had hoped. In fact, I pretty much bungled it from the start."

"I'm sorry, Nancy. It's never easy when these things don't turn out like we had hoped."

"Thanks, June. The thing is, I believe we only meet a handful of people who we instantly know are going to mean something profound to us, and she was one of them for me. I fell in love at first sight. You know, looking back, I can only recall it happening with this intensity once before, and that was with Beth."

"Was that who you were with in Florida?"

"No, that was Rachael. Beth was before her."

"Oh. You never mentioned Beth before."

My beautiful, quirky Beth. A petite woman with wild, long dark brown hair and deep blue eyes that made you dream of tropical waters. Beth could grab a hold of you with the flash of her smile. And the fact was she owned me completely.

And when Beth died, I died too.

"Ah, yes, well, that's some ancient history," I said. "The point is Brynn brought out feelings in me like I once had for Beth."

June looked compassionately at me but didn't say anything. It was as if she knew I needed space to finish, to find the strength to make the admission that hung like a pregnant pause in the conversation.

"I don't think she is going to call. I think it's too late for me."

"Oh, Nancy, you don't know that. Life is funny; it is always shifting. Things that seem lost come back, and people have a way of coming back as well. It just might be different."

The sky now was more dark than purple. With our beers finished it was time to end this conversation and call it a day.

"I believe we have a dinner waiting for us." June said.

I smiled, "Sounds perfect."

The next day started very well, with June and the other customers competing successfully on their horses. Since it was the last day of competition and our stay in Santa Fe, it was time to dismantle our temporary home and pack it all up in the trailer. I planned to leave around four a.m. to return to Tucson before the brutal summer heat reached its zenith.

Still no return call or text from Brynn. I sighed and started the mindless task of packing up. As I went through the motions, my mind wandered, and before I knew it I was thinking back on my life after Beth. Those were dark times, full of hopelessness and despair. Eventually I met Rachael, and we moved in together. But my heart wasn't in it and Rachael knew it. It was the catalyst for all our fights. And when my heart did awake it wasn't for her. What little love we had between us turned into hate.

I had a few brief affairs after Rachael before I met Maren. A mutual friend introduced us, and we hit it off instantly. Maren was always put together. Never a hair out of place, clothes perfectly pressed, and her makeup meticulously applied. I was none of those things.

We were both in transitional phases of our lives. Maren finally accepted her sexuality and separated from her husband. But she was a troubled soul trying to reconcile her desire to love women with her expectations and obligations of her family. We enjoyed each other's company and I even thought at one point this could be a serious relationship, but it didn't turn out that way. And even with Maren I still had my separateness. Then Brynn stepped into my life, and everything changed.

※※※※※※※※

I recalled the details like it was yesterday. It was early summer, and I was tagging along with Maren on a road trip to Santa Fe. It was an awkward trip. We were navigating away from being lovers and trying to move into a platonic friendship. We were only marginally successful in our attempts.

I had arranged to meet up with a friend in Santa Fe and asked her to join me on the trip. After my divorce, I relocated my business from Florida to Colorado. When your world falls apart, it's good to be around family. I had been working long hours to get my business established or at least able to pay the bills, so a weekend road trip through the Southern Colorado Rockies into Northern New Mexico sounded like a wonderful break.

It was a soft summer evening in Santa Fe, and Maren's friend Tasha had taken us to an LGBTQ happy hour. Not knowing anyone, I had the luxury of candid observation. I was staring at everything. I had never been to anything like this. It was all so beautiful, so perfect, like a movie set. I couldn't believe my good fortune.

Tasha had gone off to say hello to some of her friends, so Maren and I were standing alone, looking at the crowd. I noticed a small group of women standing about twenty feet from us. They looked so chic and sophisticated. One of the women looked over and caught my eye. She smiled and turned back to her friends. My heart leapt into my throat, and I quickly averted my eyes. I gathered my composure, and when I looked up, I saw that she had left the group and was walking toward us.

"Hi, I'm Brynn. I just wanted to say I couldn't help but notice you two. Are you new to Santa Fe?" she asked.

To say she was beautiful would be inadequate. She was stunning. A shawl was wrapped around her shoulders; underneath it was a colorful shirt with a low neckline tucked into white capris. My eyes wandered down her body and well-toned legs to her high-heeled sandals, which encased perfectly manicured toes. Her dark brown eyes contrasted with her short blonde hair. As I looked into those eyes, I felt enveloped by her.

I blinked and looked away. How long had I been staring? To my relief, I heard Maren say, "No, we are just visiting."

"Well, welcome to Santa Fe. How did you find out about this event?"

Maren explained, and it turned out that Brynn and Tasha knew each other well. We all exchanged small talk about where we were from and what we all did for a living. I found her forthright but witty, and the more she talked, the more enchanted I became.

"So, I don't know what you all have planned after this, but if you are open to it, some friends of mine own a small market down the road from here and are inviting a few people to join them there for a bite to eat. Would you like to join us?" she asked as she gestured over to the group of women.

"Absolutely!" I blurted out.

Maren shot me a look that unmistakably said *shut up*. "I don't know. See, we're here with Tasha, and I think she had something else she wanted to do this evening."

Inwardly I groaned. I wasn't aware that there were any hard plans for the evening. *Come on, Maren. This sounds amazing, don't spoil this*, I thought.

Just then, Tasha came back. "Hey, Brynn. How are you?"

"Hi, Tasha. I was just inviting Maren and Nancy, and you too, of course, to join us at the market for a bite to eat. But Maren told me you all had other plans for the evening."

"Oh, nothing this good. Yeah, that would be great. Thanks for inviting us."

"Perfect, we are probably going to be heading there in the next five or ten minutes, so see you there," she said with a smile.

Tesuque Market turned out to be a funky old wooden building located at a wide spot on the road going into Tesuque Village. I loved it instantly. It was a mix of café, bar, and small food market. The outer walls folded open which gave the place a wonderful indoor-outdoor atmosphere. There was a large group of women seated around two long tables. Everyone was having a good time, and the atmosphere was boisterous. The evening passed luxuriously as we ate, drank, and bantered with our new friends.

This is going down as one of my favorite nights of all time, I thought with a smile as I sat, full of good food, comfortably buzzed, surrounded by unique, beautiful, and intelligent women. Brynn and I had spent much of the evening close to each other, and even though she told me that she was involved with someone else, my infatuation with her had only strengthened. I longed for more of her.

Eventually, people started to leave for the night. As we got ready to leave, I moved closer to Brynn. "Thank you again for this incredible evening. I have never been around such amazing women in such beautiful surroundings."

"So glad you could join us. It's a wonderful community here."

I felt myself shake inside, fearing what I wanted to tell her, afraid of overstepping. Before I lost my nerve, I heard myself stammer out, "I am especially glad I got to know you, and hope we stay in touch."

Brynn smiled and looked deeply into my eyes. "I am too. We have each other's phone numbers, so yes, let's stay in touch. I'd like that very much."

I smiled as I watched her leave. I felt a hand on my arm and looked to see one of the women staring kindly at me.

"It was so great to meet you. I hope we see more of you here in Santa Fe."

"Oh, thank you! Yes, I hope to be back more too," I said, looking back at the door from which Brynn had just left.

The lady looked intently at me. "I see you met Brynn. She is such a wonderful person." Then, with a sly look, she added, "Shame about her breaking up with her partner. But it just wasn't the right relationship for her. Still, you never know what comes about from such things. Oh dear, look at the time. How did it get so late? I'm going to say goodnight and once again, so lovely to meet you. I hope you come back down here more."

My face must have betrayed my bewilderment. I mumbled my goodnights and confirmed my intent to return soon. As I left with my group, I was in another dimension, delirious as I attempted to understand what I had just heard. The only thing I knew with certainty was that I wanted Brynn.

⊠⊠⊠⊠⊠⊠⊠⊠⊠⊠⊠⊠

I raised my forearm to wipe the sweat off my forehead as I refocused on the present and my current task of dismantling my temporary tack room. *That was a fantastic night.* It also felt like a lifetime ago, before a series of stupid mistakes.

I snipped a zip tie around a piece of wood used for framing the curtain drapes around the tack room. I heard a pop and the board flew into my face, knocking me backward off the step-stool. Luckily, our golf cart was right behind me. I fell into it. I heard June gasp.

"Oh! Oh my!" she exclaimed. "Nancy, are you okay? What happened?"

I slumped onto the seat. My lower lip felt tingly. I brought my hand up to my mouth. It felt wet. As I took my hand away, I saw blood. *Seriously?* I grabbed a towel from the golf cart and pressed it to my lip.

June came over, and the look on her face told me everything I needed to know. Wisely, she just kept silent. Tears streamed down my face as I sat there holding a bloody rag to my mouth. I was beaten and battered. Everything brought me to this numbed-out state: reliving my past mistakes for two straight weeks, the stress and physical toll of constant travel and competitions, and the inevitable fatigue from such an ambitious schedule. I felt like an untethered boat in a storm, bashing on the moorings.

"I'm okay," I said finally. I attempted to smile. "I told you two weeks in Santa Fe was a bad idea."

June moved to the front of the golf cart and looked straight at me. I looked at her eyes and saw their expression shift from concern to compassion. I first noticed her shoulders shaking, then her head. Eventually, her whole body shook. She started to laugh.

"Oh my God, what else could happen to you here?" she laughed. "First your heart, then food poisoning, and now you have a split lip."

The absurdity of it all was laid before us, and I felt myself lighten as I joined her laughter. She was right, and once again, she helped me to let go and find joy in the moment. Or at least the humor of it. And although it hurt and definitely didn't help the bleeding, I let go and laughed to the point of tears.

June looked intently into my eyes and, with all seriousness, said, "You need a vacation."

WHY IRELAND?

Ireland?" Julie asked. "Why Ireland?"

"I love Ireland. It's so beautiful," Donna said.

Undaunted, Julie continued with her interrogation. "But why are you going alone?"

I was having dinner with three of my friends, and I had told them my decision. Liane sat silently at the table, watching. I had told her earlier, so she wasn't surprised.

"I need a vacation, and I've been wanting to go back," I replied.

I decided to return to Ireland during my drive from Santa Fe to Tucson. The idea came to me during the long hours alone on the road, and once the thought had taken hold, there was no going back.

The truth was I longed to return. Two years prior, I had gone to Ireland and taken my elderly parents. It was wonderful to share that experience with them, but it felt incomplete. The Island was not done with me, nor I with her.

I had been back from Santa Fe for a month, and the emptiness I felt there had still not gone away. In fact, it was more intense. The realization of finally losing Brynn played upon my mind. I should have reached out better. I should have apologized for my stupid behavior. Or maybe I should have been smart enough to know I had bungled it up beyond repair. I had no good answers. The only thing that made any sense was that I needed to find myself again. I needed to heal.

I realized the table was silent, and Julie stared at me with an expectant look.

"I'm sorry, what did you say?" I asked.

"I have friends in Liverpool. I'm going to call them and let them know you are coming," Julie said with blunt conviction.

"But I'm not going to Liverpool," I replied incredulously.

"Fine, go to Dublin and then go stay with my friends. They are super nice and will show you around. It's just a short ferry ride."

"Julie, I'm not going to Liverpool. And I'm not going to spend my trip with people I don't know," I said. She always pushed me to do what she wanted, and I was fed up with it.

Julie shot back, "Well, it's stupid to go by yourself. You're going to be lonely with no one to talk to. And besides, it's too dangerous to travel alone."

I sighed, "Julie, it's Ireland. Besides, you do realize that I just spent the last three months driving alone with a trailer full of horses all over the western United States. I think I know how to handle myself and stay safe."

"Fine!" Julie shouted. "Just go. Do whatever you want. Be selfish. I could care less. But this doesn't make you interesting or independent or whatever bullshit you are telling yourself."

Sensing the explosion that was about to erupt from my mouth, Liane broke her silence. "Julie, it's her trip. Leave it alone."

"Yeah, I love traveling by myself," Donna chimed in. "Some of my best trips have been solo." Realizing she was outnumbered, Julie let it go. The rest of the dinner passed amicably, and we all said our goodnights.

I was awakened early the next morning to my phone ringing.

"Good God," I groaned. "What time is it?" I looked at the clock: 6.00 a.m. I saw that the caller was Julie and let it go to voicemail. I was done. Instead of making me second-guess my decision, Julie's outburst had left me more resolved. This was exactly why I needed to change my life. I needed to take it back and not give a damn if it met with anyone's approval.

I decided to leave in a couple of weeks. As I started to plan it out, it soon became apparent that I was going to the southeast quadrant of Ireland called the Ancient East. I loved history and looked forward to immersing myself in museums and ancient ruins. At my core, I was just a big geek, and no matter how hard I tried all these years, the fact was that I just wasn't one of the cool kids. My time in Santa Fe made that clear. But something else was also beckoning me, something elusive but nonetheless compelling. I needed to go there. I needed to know more about who I am and who my people are. What is my culture? The things I used to identify with no longer served me, and I felt lost.

I thought about my paternal great-grandfather, John Britt. He immigrated to the US from Ireland, but that was the only thing I knew about him. He was a pariah in the family. No stories were told of him, and my past attempts to elicit information about him from my grandfather were met with indifference and dismissal. In later years, I tried again to learn more from my father, but he just confessed ignorance and disinterest.

It had always struck me as odd that a family so proud of its Irish heritage was dismissive of the closest blood connection we had to the Island. John Britt was *persona non grata* as far as my grandfather had been concerned. What makes a son disinherit his father?

Abuse was the first and most obvious issue that came to mind, but I suspected there was more. My curiosity led me to attempt a genealogy search with one of the online companies, yet even that was stonewalled quickly as I got no further than knowing who he'd married. Nothing was consistent about the man, not even his age.

Perhaps the only relevant thing I had learned was that he was born after the harshest episodes of the Irish Potato Famine. I tried to visualize the devastation he experienced. The harsh survivalism that existed among those who lived. The desperation to escape, to forget the horrors that surrounded him. As he lay in a bunk of a coffin ship, did he dream of a land that would make it all go away?

Then, when he finally made it to the United States and had a farm of his own in Iowa, did he look out on those vast open plains, and instead of golden wheat fields, did his mind's eye see the rolling green hills of Ireland? And did he cry?

Was such trauma passed down through the generations? Did I carry a sorrow from my ancestors that now manifested itself in ways

I could not yet understand? I did not know. All I knew was that I needed answers, and my soul told me to go to Ireland.

So, I booked my flight and arranged my hotels in Dublin. I had a place to stay at the beginning and the end, and the rest was up for grabs. My parents had taught me to travel this way. It was exciting not to know where I was going to end up at the end of the day. I might sleep in the car for the night, but I was willing to take that risk in exchange for the freedom it offered.

I needed an adventure, not an itinerary.

SAN FRANCISCO

My plane out of Phoenix touched down in San Francisco just before 8:00 a.m. I had an eight-hour layover, but I didn't care. I welcomed the time alone and was anxious to start my adventure.

During the flight, I'd had another episode with my heart. The pain intensified as the plane accelerated into the sky, and I broke into a cold sweat. "*Good God,*" I thought, "*am I going to have an in-flight emergency?*" Fortunately, the pain started to subside as the plane leveled off. With trepidation, I silently cursed myself for not dealing with it after Santa Fe and wondered if I would have to cancel the trip. I prayed it was just a bad case of heartburn.

After some water and a package of pretzels I started to feel better. I looked out the window and thought, *It's going to take more than that for me to turn back.*

As soon as I disembarked, I made a beeline to a newsstand kiosk and got some antacids. Now I needed to find a place to hang out and get something to eat. Thirty minutes later, with a Danish and coffee in hand, I found a comfy lounge chair and settled in. I pulled out my journal from my last trip to Ireland and read back through it.

Happy memories filled me as I relived that trip. I felt blessed that I was allowed to join my parents. Laughter escaped me as I read about my first experience driving on the left side of the road. I remembered how terrified I was and how every time cars came at me, I had to fight the urge to swerve out of my lane, convinced I was on the wrong side of the road. I chuckled as I recalled the bedlam of my eighty-five-year-old father, who was trying to navigate while he cursed at the map, other drivers, and my mother (as if she had any influence over his inability to read the map). We all white-knuckled it that day and other days too. I closed my journal and started to watch all the people around me. Airports are the best places to people-watch. I saw dozens of folks rushing past to get to their connecting flight. Parents were burdened with multiple overstuffed bags filled with items for their small children, who were intent on going in whatever direction would cause their parents the most chaos. I looked at them with pity. The amount of stuff needed to travel with children baffled me. To me, it looked as if they were taking a two-week trek through the Himalayas instead of a few hours in an airplane. As I looked at the moving mass of humanity, I became conscious of my solitude. I didn't necessarily mind it, but I did reflect, sadly, on the lack of a companion to share my life with.

I began to ponder my ideal companion, and then I thought of Brynn. I quickly stopped myself. *No,* I told myself, *this journey is meant to be done alone.* I needed to discover myself, and until I did that, any preconceived ideas of who I wanted to be with were just that, *preconceived.*

Before I could mentally change the subject matter, my phone rang. I saw it was a very dear friend of mine from Florida.

"Guess where I am?" I said happily.

"Up Shits Creek without a paddle," she answered.

We both laughed. Paula was one of my closest friends, and her craziness was a huge factor in keeping me sane. Her irreverent humor and sarcasm always left me in pain from laughing way too much.

"How are you? I see Florida keeps dodging the hurricanes." I had lived in Florida for thirteen years and dreaded every hurricane season.

"Very true, Yoda." She laughed. Paula had a nickname for most things and people, and Yoda was mine.

"I'm here with an Angry in my hand, contemplating the need to change my underwear for the third time today because it's so fucking humid, and wondering what would be the most inconspicuous way to kill my husband, and then I thought, I need to talk to you. How are you?"

Angry was the nickname for her favorite cider. Her other favorite beverages included bourbon, red wine, tequila, and most things alcoholic.

"I'm sitting in the San Francisco airport waiting to fly out to Ireland," I boasted.

A howl of laughter erupted on the phone. Not the response I was expecting.

"What's so funny about that?" I asked.

"I hope you brought your waders. *You're* the one flying into a fucking hurricane!"

"Wait. What?"

"Yep, and it's a big one too, if I remember correctly. Let me look at the paper here," she laughed. I heard her move about and the rustle of a newspaper. "Yep, its name is Lorenzo, and…" Paula was now laughing hysterically. "Oh, and it's a Category Five."

"Nooooo!" I moaned into the phone. People seated by me shot sideways glances, obviously wondering what mental illness I was suffering from. *Just my luck to be flying into a hurricane!*

We laughed and joked some more about my impeccable timing. Eventually we said our goodbyes, and she wished me well on my trip.

I made my way to the gate. Despite my best intentions to make it a leisurely stroll, I felt myself caught up in the rushing tide of humanity, and my step picked up pace as I strove to keep up with those around me. Years of conditioning drove me to keep up for fear of being left behind, even though, rationally, there was nothing or no one to keep up with.

I'd been running to keep up my whole life. Being the youngest of four children with a significant age gap between myself and the other three, I always felt a certain degree of isolation and exclusion from their inner circle. They were all so cool in my mind, and I was the awkward child constantly wishing to be included in their adventures. I was literally running after them, hoping to be included in whatever they were doing. Even now, five decades later, I still couldn't shake this feeling.

I made it to my gate and settled in for the wait. I pulled my journal out again and started to write down the day's events so far. I mused over what I wanted to experience on this trip. Besides just enjoying being there, I wanted to get past the stereotypes. But mostly I wanted to find a personal connection with my ancestral homeland. I yearned to connect to something on a soul level. I needed an anchor to ground me. And even though I had been brought up to identify as Irish, I didn't fully understand what that meant. It had to be more substantial than the ability to consume copious amounts of alcohol and a predisposition for a fiery temper.

So, I wanted to explore Ireland's roots, especially its early history. Perhaps by going back to the early beginnings, I too would find my foundation. On my first trip to Ireland with my parents, I took them to see the Book of Kells at Trinity College in Dublin. They weren't into it that much, so our trip through the exhibit was very cursory. This time, I planned to take as much time as I wanted. I wanted to soak it in. I wanted to understand its importance. I knew there was a depth of culture that I hadn't reconnected to, just as I knew there was more depth to me that I hadn't allowed myself to connect to. I needed to find it.

Would I be able to do that? Would I even know what it is I needed to find? Perhaps I was too flawed to find enlightenment. Perhaps I was too damaged. Perhaps I was too unworthy. I sat in the airport chair and stared out at the tarmac.

My mind started to shuffle through the index cards of my failures. My regrets of lost chances, of risks not taken because I wasn't strong enough to accept failure or, more pointedly, success. My shame of being dishonest at times when I wished I had been brave enough to stand my ground, especially when I was in the wrong. Why was I so willing to accept the construct that I would fail at whatever I wanted the most, but not willing to accept the idea that

I was just as able and worthy as anyone else to have success, love, comfort, and most of all, happiness?

Now I was sitting alone in an airport, waiting to board a plane to take me on a trip that I hoped would fix all of this. My self-doubts continued their assault, and I wondered whether this was just another delusional expectation that was doomed to fail and thus just affirm my inability to rise above it all, to grow, to have that epiphany that changes one for the better. Maybe Julie was right, and this was just a pathetic attempt to appear interesting and nothing more. Maybe I really was just a self-centered asshole, doomed to live a life of self-denial and sabotage.

I stared out at the overcast sky. I sighed and shifted in my chair. An Aer Lingus plane was approaching the gate. This was my plane. The area around me was filled with people deboarding and moving off into the airport. There were fewer empty seats at the gate as more and more people arrived for the next flight. A small group of young professionals sat down around me. They were laughing and joking, and I found their enthusiasm infectious.

As I eavesdropped on their conversation, it became clear they were going to some sort of software conference in Dublin. I soon found myself engaging with them about their trip, and they in turn asked me about mine. Their enthusiasm lifted me out of my funk, and I felt the return of my optimism. As I laughed and joked with the group, I thought to myself, *Who knows how it will all turn out, but come hell or high water, I'm going to go for it. No expectations, no judgment on the outcome, and let's see what happens.*

BRYNN

I stopped my story to prepare dinner. I was standing at the grill cooking salmon when Jen broke her silence.

"You never mentioned Brynn before," she said.

"No, I haven't. God's truth, I am ashamed of how I handled or, more accurately, didn't handle my boorish actions the last time I saw her," I answered.

Jen refilled our wine glasses. "By that, I'm assuming you're referencing the 'drunk off your ass' moment. Tell me about it."

I took a deep breath. I realized if I wanted Jen to understand, I had to tell the whole story; it was time I confessed.

"It happened the previous summer when I was up in Santa Fe, again at a horse show. It was a tough time. It was my first season back in the show ring after my leg injury, and I had an especially difficult customer. I could tell she was looking for a reason to fire me. Well, that just fed into my worst insecurities. I tried and tried to make her happy. In fact, her horse was doing really well, but I was still weak. My best friends, who were also trainers in New Mexico, were helping me by doing the actual show riding. I did the prep work, they showed the horse, and all was going very well. But there were other trainers interested in keeping her dissatisfied. Knowing you are undergoing character assassination and not being able to stop it..." I paused as the emotions of that experience resurfaced. I swallowed hard and continued. "Well, it was a horrible experience."

Jen sat silently, giving me the space to regroup and continue.

"It was the second-to-last day, and that evening I had made arrangements to meet Brynn for dinner. I was so excited about it. Well, that day there was some special event, and my customers wanted me to go with them. This difficult customer made it clear

33

that she wanted me to be there; it was more like an ultimatum. I don't know why it was so important to her. But I knew the vultures were circling, and I needed to protect my clientele if I hoped to have any business left by the morning. I told them I would go, but that I was going to have to leave early because I had plans that evening."

"Is it really that cutthroat?" Jen asked.

"It can be. I hadn't really had much trouble that way before. But I was just coming back from a debilitating injury. I had completely severed a tendon in my leg, and I wasn't really up to full speed. In fact, I wasn't sure I would ever be able to ride like I used to. So there were plenty of opportunities for other trainers to make it clear they could do a better job than me."

I pulled the salmon from the grill and walked back into the house. Jen followed.

"Anyway, I went to this event, and everyone was drinking and partying like hell. It was the end of the show circuit and we were all letting down our guard and having fun. It was a sport horse auction. Neither I nor my clients had any interest in purchasing, so I ignored all the demonstration rides going on. I did have fun talking and joking with everyone. But I was keeping an eye on the time.

"I don't really know how, but suddenly everything seemed to go out of control. It started with someone grabbing my arm and escorting me into the VIP section. Why? I don't know. But I was, and my customers were brought in too. In a blink of an eye, I had champagne in my hand and was seated at a table with a clear view of the auction area.

"My problem customer was thoroughly enjoying the experience and I thought, stupidly, that maybe if I just humored her a bit all would be okay. I looked at the time and realized that I wasn't going to make my dinner with Brynn. It was about two hours until our planned meet-up time, but I still needed to go back to the hotel and clean up. So I texted Brynn and apologized and let her know I was still hung up at the show. We agreed to put it back an hour. She was so wonderful, so understanding. I feel like an even bigger shit as I tell you this now."

Jen laughed. "Yep. This is sounding like a big fuck-up."

"Oh yeah, and it gets better. So, I sat at this table, teasing another trainer about how she should buy this horse or that horse, and all the while my champagne glass didn't seem to go down. I have little tolerance for wine or champagne on the best of days, but after being in the sun all day with little to eat, not indulging in alcohol for two weeks, and all the stress I was feeling, well, I was doomed.

"Now, true disaster is about to strike. At this point, I felt really relaxed but not drunk. Then a friend popped out of nowhere and put her head between me and June and said, 'if you can get this next horse for less than $6,500, that is a great deal.'

"Well, I was drunk, so I thought, *This is a great idea.* I looked at June, and she laughed and said okay. So, I started bidding on the horse. I didn't know anything about this horse. But I trusted my friend. Long story short, I won the bid, and we now own another horse. I was thinking, *okay, don't panic, worst case scenario I'll improve it and we can sell it.*"

"Oh my God! That was really gutsy of you." Jen looked at me in disbelief.

I laughed. "Actually, it was completely asinine for me to do that. Once the bidding was done, they wanted all the successful bidders to come down on the field and get their picture taken with the horses. June didn't want any part of that, so my friend and I went down. Now, I knew I was drunk. I also knew I needed to get out of there so I could meet Brynn at the restaurant. But I couldn't leave until I did this.

"So, we went down and they brought up this small bay mare. I thought *Oh crap, it's a mare and she is small.* And I mean really small for a horse. Almost pony-sized. *Okay, game face on, my friend wouldn't steer me wrong. It'll be okay.'* I walked to the mare's right side, and my heart dropped. Horrified, I looked at her right eye and saw it's all cloudy. *Oh, My God! What have I done? She's blind in that eye.* The earth and sky were spinning faster and faster as I realized how badly I'd just fucked up!

"I looked at my friend and just let loose. 'What the fuck did you just get me into?' She came over and saw what I was talking about. Her face was ashen too. At this time the daughter of the family running the auction of their horses came up and overheard my meltdown. She rightly said that this was disclosed in the brochure. Of course, it was. I just didn't see it because I had no intention of buying a horse."

"What did you do?" Jen asked.

"I panicked. I grabbed my friend and said 'What did you do to me? Oh my God! I got one customer almost out the door and now I just had June buy a blind horse!' To my friend's credit, she stood by her claim.

"Now I was seriously late for making my dinner date with Brynn. I wasn't going to be able to clean up. I had to leave everyone and pretend that, 'wow it's all so great,' all the while I was freaking out inside. I drove out of the showground and pulled over before I got to the main road. I opened the door and promptly threw up.

"What a screw-up. I never should have been driving. And I should have had the decency to tell her I totally messed up. Instead, I freaked out and thought I had to salvage something, and I desperately wanted to salvage my night with her."

Jen swirled her wine glass and looked thoughtfully into it. I stayed silent. I had no defense for my actions. I looked at my plate, ready for the condemnation. Eventually, Jen took a sip and looked at me.

"What happened next?" Jen asked without judgment.

"I drove up to El Dorado to meet her. I was in full panic mode. I realized I had screwed up on every level. With June, with Brynn, with myself.

"Eventually, I made it to the restaurant. Brynn was waiting and was so gracious. I confessed my inebriation, but I couldn't explain to her why I was. I just couldn't accept or understand why I allowed everything to get so out of control.

"Well, dinner was a complete mess. I couldn't eat. I could barely follow the conversation. My mind bounced between how badly I screwed up the afternoon at the auction and how badly I was screwing up my dinner with Brynn.

"I just proved to everyone that day how fucked up I was. I apologized profusely to Brynn that night and the next day. She was very cool about it and said it was no big deal. But it was. And the fact is I didn't, and I still haven't, forgiven myself for that night."

"And what did you do about the horse and June?" Jen asked.

"As I drove home from dinner, I made the decision to just come clean with June in the morning. I was going to offer to pay her back, and I hoped that would be enough for her to forgive me.

"Early the next day, I told her.

"She just looked me straight in the eye and said 'no.' She realized that the school horse needed to retire soon, and this horse could fill his shoes. I broke down inside. I was so grateful. For her understanding, for her compassion, and most of all for her belief in our future."

"Wow, that was incredibly understanding of her," Jen stated.

"It was. Now I'm going to tell you a funny side story. That Christmas, when June and I exchanged gifts, she had this glint in her eye as she handed me her present. It was a square box, and inside were four champagne flutes. June was laughing, and as I looked closely at them, I realized they were the glasses from the auction. She took them. I laughed. It was then that I knew for certain all was good between us. I might have been drunk-bidding, but June was stealing the stemware."

DAY ONE

DUBLIN

It was overcast and raining when we touched down. People were up and retrieving their carry-ons. I remained seated. I had no agenda other than getting to my hotel and no timetable in which to make that happen.

Eventually, I exited the plane and began the long walk up to Customs. I looked out the large glass walls at the grey skies of Dublin, and my heart was full of joy. For some inexplicable reason it felt more like a homecoming rather than the start of a vacation.

I got to the Customs area and queued up. The line was long but moved quickly, and eventually, I handed my passport to the official. He flipped through my book and noticed I had visited two years previously. He looked at me with a deadpan expression.

"What brings you to Ireland? Business?" he asked.

"No, strictly pleasure, I'm taking a vacation."

"Arizona. Hmm, it's pretty hot there."

"Yes, I'm looking forward to the rain," I said teasingly.

My joke fell flat as he looked down at my passport and then back up at me. He did this a couple of times, and I began to feel a bit nervous. Eventually, he decided I wasn't a terrorist or refugee or whatever and stamped my book.

In an abrupt turn around he smiled and handed me back my passport. "Have a good vacation."

Relieved that was over, I made my way out of the airport and found the taxi queue. The line moved quickly, and in a few minutes, I had a cab. It was a woman driver, and I gave her the address for the hotel. A drizzle had started as we drove south into the city. In my experience, I have found cab drivers to be friendly and curious, and she immediately asked me why I was there.

"I'm here on holiday. Actually, it's my first trip by myself," I answered.

"Oh, how brave. I'd never be able to do that," she stated. "But oh, that does sound like a lot of fun. What made you decide to come by yourself?"

I thought about her question and wondered what response would be appropriate. *Should I just say I needed a vacation and didn't have anyone special in my life because I keep fucking up relationships? Should I tell her that I feel a deep soul connection to this place and the Island called me back? Should I tell her I'm desperate to find meaning in my life, and I hope this trip will give it to me? Or should I just find a quick surface reply and leave it at that?*

I noticed that we were around the same age. "I was here a couple of years ago with my parents, and while I loved that trip, I left wanting to come back by myself to explore a bit more. They are getting old and need more and more help, so I decided this might be my last chance to travel for a while."

"Oh, I hear ye. My da passed a couple of years ago, God bless him, and now I got my mam to care for. It's so hard as they age. I have my brother, but mam lives with me and the kids. It's tight. Good for you for taking some time now, because when you lose one, or they get seriously ill, you just got to be there for them."

We are all in the same boat, I thought. looking out the window.

"Sorry to hear about your dad. I'm lucky I've got both of my parents, but they are getting frail, and I worry about how I'm going to help them through this stage of life. So since I work for myself, I decided to take some time off and come here to explore my Irish roots."

"What do you do?"

"Believe it or not, people pay me to ride their horses and teach them," I replied.

I felt an energy shift, and I noticed her eyes fire up as she looked into the rearview mirror back at me. "Really? That's so great. Me and my brother rode as kids. My da would put shoes on people's horses, what's that called?"

"He was a farrier, or do you call them blacksmiths? Awesome! Did he do that for a living?" I asked as I leaned forward.

"Oh no! But he knew how, ye see, because he grew up on a farm and his da showed him. We lived north of here in a small town. Not much to brag about, and people struggled to make it. So my da would help them, and he wouldn't take no money. No, he wouldn't. Because he knew. He knew they couldn't pay. And he knew those ponies needed it. He would just do it for free to help them, ye see. He was always helping others. He was so great. He knew, he just knew. People would let me and my brother ride, so ye see all was good."

The love and pride in her voice as she talked about her father and where she grew up was unmistakable. I listened to her talk about the town where she grew up and how much fun she and her brother had. She spoke of her dad's generosity and how hard he worked. It was clear she was well cared for, but there were no extras.

As we got closer to the city center, the roads noticeably narrowed, and traffic became even more congested as cars and trucks navigated the maze of streets. Eventually, we arrived at the hotel on a narrow one-way street. I thanked her and entered the hotel.

I was early for check-in, but the hotel would hold my bag. Two young clerks were working, and both exuded a warmth and friendliness that was disarming.

"Hey, where would be a good place to get a bite to eat?" I asked.

The young man looked up. "What are you in the mood for? There are lots of great places to eat nearby."

"Oh, just some simple pub food," I replied. Mostly, I wanted a pint of Guinness.

"Well, the Hairy Lemon can't be beaten, and it's just right there across the street," he said with a smile.

The young girl seconded that opinion, so I thanked them and set off. Now I felt like I was on vacation, and my step lightened as I set out across the street.

The Hairy Lemon had a charming pub atmosphere of dark wood, cozy tables tucked about, and various memorabilia on the walls. I went to the restaurant section and was seated so that I had a view of the other patrons and the windows looking out onto the street. As I ate my lunch and sipped my Guinness, I noticed a young couple seated diagonally from me, looking at their travel books and planning their next sightseeing adventure. Next to them was a single woman who looked like she was on a lunch break, reading a book as she ate. Across the room and directly in front of me were two women around my age, one with what looked like a glass of white zinfandel and the other with a pint of Guinness, their heads close together in deep conversation. I wondered if they were lovers and felt a pang of solitude as I gazed at them.

I shifted my attention and looked out of the windows. It was raining hard now, and I watched people scurry quickly about, mostly with umbrellas. I caught the waitress' attention and motioned her over.

"All done?" she asked.

"Just about," I replied. "Actually, I have a question for you. If you were leaving work right now and didn't have an umbrella, where would you go close by to get one?"

She smiled, "Oh, go to Dunnes. It's just over at Stephen's Green."

"Stephen's Green?" I asked.

"It's a shopping center just over there." She gestured diagonally out of the window. "You can't miss it."

I thanked her and paid my bill. I set off as she instructed. It was ridiculously close, just like she said. This was a good thing, because in the short distance I walked, I was fairly soaked. I entered the shopping center off King Street. As I entered the main area, my eyes were drawn up to the amazing glass and steel enclosure of the center. It was beautiful and created an open feeling even on a cloudy, rainy day.

I decided to quickly pop into Dunnes to get an umbrella and then explore the building more. As I wandered about trying to figure out where to find an umbrella, I felt less and less like a tourist. I browsed through the clothing racks. Eventually, I found the umbrellas and set out to explore the rest of the center. Not being much of a shopper, I chose to go to the top floor and take pictures. I walked around looking at the people and various shop signs. When I reached the other end, I saw there was a famine exhibit. It was still too early to go back to the hotel, so I decided to check it out.

It was a self-guided tour, and I was stunned by how much I didn't know about this episode of Irish history. In a span of about four years, one million people died in Ireland, and a million more had emigrated. What I didn't know was the extent to which the British government sought to block aid and how some saw it as a solution to the "Irish problem." I grew angrier and angrier as I read accounts of evictions and looked at photographs of battering rams used to destroy family homes. The destitution in the eyes of the people seared into my soul. I thought of my great-grandfather, John Britt, and how much anger he must have had in him.

I finished with the exhibit and walked back to the hotel. The rain was still coming down steadily, and I was glad I had the umbrella. But coming from the hot Arizona desert, I was chilled through to the bone and was looking forward to a hot bath.

I got my bag and room key and headed up in the elevator to my room on the third floor. It was a spacious room with large windows that disappointingly looked out onto an alley. However, the bathroom was modern and clean, with a full-sized tub. A few minutes later, with a cup of hot tea in my hand, I was blissfully soaking in a steaming hot bath.

I leaned back in the tub and closed my eyes. As I felt the warmth slowly envelop me, my thoughts turned back to the famine exhibit. The Irish Famine victims would have been classified as refugees in today's world.

These are my people. This is part of who I am. This is my culture.

How is this type of trauma resolved generationally? Is it? I never felt the emotional impact of the famine, or The Great Hunger, until today. In a land so fertile, it was despicable that the people were not able to eat the wheat and barley because it was being shipped abroad to England. The cattle, sheep, and pigs were also sold off. Protestant missionaries used food to coerce Catholics to convert, a practice known as "taking the soup."

Hunger is an enemy that demoralizes you. There is nothing to fight against, and time is its weapon. Those who are desperate cling to hope and pray that mercy will be given. But hunger has no compassion, and hope was a great betrayer as successive potato crops failed.

With my eyes still closed, I soaked in the hot water, my stomach full, and the cold driven out of my bones. Comfortable and safe, far removed from the horrors that occurred one hundred and seventy-four years ago, I drifted into a semiconscious state. As I lay there a soft voice whispered.

Nursemaid I was
as both suckled at my breasts,
brothers born of different mothers.
Proudly, their father would gaze upon them,
knowing each would grow to be great men
and share in his kingdom.

With a father's love, the kingdom was split

and they lived in different houses.
But in their separateness, they grew jealous,
envious of the love and abundance their father bestowed
on the other.

They coveted each other's lands, wives, cattle, and horses,
and so their bitterness grew into hatred, and that hatred
took over their memories.

Such that they forgot the time when they were brothers,
asleep in each other's arms,
content from the richness of my milk.

I bolted upright in the tub, startled by the woman's voice with its soft Irish accent. I looked around the empty bathroom. Silence.

"What just happened?" I asked myself out loud.

Quickly, I got out of the bathtub and wrapped myself in a towel. I stepped into the main area, looking about cautiously. But the room was empty, and the door was still locked. I was alone.

As I got dressed, I realized that I must have dozed off in the tub. What I thought was a voice speaking to me must have been my subconscious taking over.

Yes. That's exactly what happened, I told myself, taking comfort in this rational explanation. Much better than believing there were mysterious voices talking to you.

I looked at myself in the bathroom mirror. Only my eyes stared back at me. Nobody and nothing else was here with me. However, as I combed through my hair, no matter how much I told myself it was irrational, I couldn't shake the feeling that for a brief moment, I had not been alone.

BETH

Warmed and refreshed, I stepped out into the cool evening air. The rain had subsided, so I decided to take a walk before getting dinner. I retraced my steps along King Street but instead of entering the shopping center, I continued until it intersected with Grafton Street. In the center of this intersection, a young white guy in dreadlocks played Hendrix's "Angel" on his guitar. A box was on the ground before him with a smattering of coins in it. I was at the south end of Grafton which abutted a major thoroughfare. Across it was St. Stephen's Green. I turned in the opposite direction and proceeded to walk north on Grafton toward Trinity College.

Grafton was alive with activity. People were scurrying about in every direction. Buskers spaced themselves out along the street, each with a box, jar, or guitar case open so people could toss in coins. I noticed that they stationed themselves in congested areas where there was a large influx of people coming in from certain side streets. Teenagers moved in segregated packs of boys and girls, each pretending to be unaware of the other.

I strolled along, taking it all in, dodging around slower walkers, moving aside for faster ones. I browsed the various shops lining the street. Restaurants and pubs were filling up as people were getting off from work and settling in for a pint or bite to eat.

I reached the north end of Grafton and decided to meander back by using the side streets. Eventually, I went down a narrow street and saw a side entrance to a church called St. Teresa's. The church bells were ringing, and I knew Mass was about to start.

I was raised by devout Roman Catholic parents. I even went to parochial school from kindergarten until my sophomore year in high school. But I was in no manner a devoted Catholic.

Since I had accepted my sexuality, I felt ostracized and abandoned by religion, by all religions. I liked to think of myself as a spiritual person, but truth be told, I really wasn't. To say God and I had a distant relationship would be more to the truth of the matter. I had been to Mass occasionally with my parents, but it had been twenty years or more since I had gone to church voluntarily. I stared at the grotto entrance that led to the church. Normally I would have continued on my way. But instead, I just stood there, conflicted.

Without any clear reason why, I turned and entered the church. I stepped into a side vestibule and found a seat on a pew toward the back. Due to my hesitation, the Mass had already started. I settled in, feeling self-conscious as the churchgoers looked at me.

The priest was a young man and I sat transfixed by his voice singing out a prayer to the congregation. The harmonics of his chanting in the lofty church stirred up powerful feelings of mysticism and humility. There was a woman sitting next to me on my right praying the rosary. I smiled and thought of my mother who also always said her rosary during Mass. I looked across the aisle and the pews and noticed the confessional boxes. People were going in and out of one of them.

I tried to listen to the readings, but my attention kept drifting back to the confessional. *The power of absolution is seductive*, I thought. *The ability to let go of misdeeds or wrongs inflicted on others through the simple act of contrition.* I had often compared it to therapy, but now I looked at it from a different perspective.

I went to therapy to address perceived wrongs done unto me, for the most part. I would sit and tell my therapist about how I was hurt, how I was wronged or misunderstood. The focus was on me and my beliefs about the situation.

But the confessional was different. Here you went to address wrongs you had done to another, or wrongs you believed you had done to God. It was the act of taking ownership of your faults, your sins, and then through true remorse seek out forgiveness and redemption. For the truly repentant, God's mercy would be bestowed and you would be absolved from your sins. I sighed. For those who believed, they must receive such comfort.

The priest rose from his seat and walked to the front of the altar. As he started in on his sermon, I thought about Beth.

We had both been raised Catholic. We had also been born in the same small West Texas town, a year apart. Our fathers worked in the oil industry in Midland, Texas, a booming oil town in the late 1960s. We didn't meet until we were in our late twenties, in Colorado. When we discovered our shared history, it bonded us instantly.

I suddenly realized it had been twenty-five years since her passing. I didn't know why, but I allowed myself to think back to that fateful day in early March.

෨෨෨෨෨෨෨෨෨෨෨෨

It was late afternoon on a beautiful spring day in Denver, Colorado. I had just returned to my house from being out all day. As I opened the front door, I heard my home phone ringing. I rushed to get it.

"Hello," I said breathlessly.

"Nancy? Hey, this is Linda."

"Hey, Linda, what's up?" I replied happily. I was in an exceptionally good mood and enjoying the nice spring day.

"Do you have a minute? I need to tell you something… important." Linda's voice started to break at the end. I could tell something was wrong, seriously wrong.

"Yeah, sure, what is it?"

There was silence on the phone, and I could tell she was crying. *Oh my God, it must be really bad.* I knew Linda had started dating someone she really liked. *Oh no,* I thought. *They broke up.*

"Beth is dead!" she blurted out.

I went numb. *I must have heard her wrong*, I told myself. Linda was sobbing on the other end, babbling about some nonsense about how she got a call from Beth's roommate up in Aspen. Nothing was making any sense.

"Wait, what did you just say?" I asked.

Linda took a deep breath. "Beth was found dead this morning." Her voice started to crack up again. "She was found drowned in the hot tub."

Now the room was spinning, and I collapsed to the floor. Linda started sobbing again. *This can't be happening, this isn't true,* I told myself. Beth was working up in Aspen as a massage therapist for the winter ski season. She roomed with some friends when she was up there.

"How?" I heard myself ask. I felt drugged and dissociated.

"I guess she had worked a lot yesterday and was really tired. They were all in the hot tub, drinking, smoking pot, and relaxing. You know how Beth loved hot baths. Well, I guess the others left her there and went to bed and…" Linda's voice trailed off, and I heard more sobbing. Eventually, she found her voice. "…and they didn't know she had drowned until they woke up this morning."

It was hard to remember the next few days. It was all a blur as the reality of her death came upon me. Beth and I had kept the depth of our relationship private from the rest of our group of friends. The intensity of our connection was intimidating, and we were too young to know how to deal with it. We certainly didn't want any of the others to know, at least not until we were sure. We scared each other but loved each other. Most of all we didn't want to lose each other, and if that meant that we would only be friends in the end, we wanted to be able to do that.

As the days passed after Linda broke the news, I kept expecting Beth to call or walk through the door, tossing her long dark brown hair as she bounced into the room. She would laugh and say there had been a misunderstanding. She was fine, and nothing was wrong. Then she would take me in her arms, look at me with her beautiful blue eyes, press her soft full lips to mine, and all would be right again. But it never happened.

I went through the days numb, unable to cry or talk about it for the fear of making it real. My friends consoled me and each other. Beth's parents came and took her back to Texas to be buried. They made it clear that it was going to be a Catholic church ceremony and none of us were invited. All I could think was how much Beth would hate all of it.

Linda decided we would have our own memorial celebration of Beth's life. We all chipped in some money and bought a sapling tree to plant in her memory in Cheesman Park, our Sunday hanging-out place. I have no idea how, but Linda got the Denver Parks Administration to agree to let us do it.

The service was crowded with many who knew Beth and had been touched by her kind and magnetic personality. Her sister Mary came, which was nice. We planted the tree, and various individuals shared their thoughts, memories, and prayers. Eventually, the service came to an end, and our group went back to Linda's house for a private gathering.

Death is a strange event for the living, I thought as we gathered. In some ways, it was as it always was when we got together. We hugged, we laughed, we drank, we smoked, and we talked about our daily lives. But this time, Beth's absence was the ghost in the room.

Everyone had a funny story to share about Beth. I stayed silent. I couldn't tell them my special story now. It didn't seem right to bring it out to the group. Our secret was my burden to bear.

I got up and went to the backyard to get another beer from the ice chest. I was alone, and I stayed out and breathed in the cool evening air. I could feel myself cracking, and the corners of my eyes felt damp. *No, don't lose it now,* I told myself.

I heard the back door open and close. I wiped my face and turned around. It was Beth's sister.

"Hi, Mary, it's nice out here," I said, trying to keep my voice steady.

"Yes, it is. Actually, I'm glad I got you alone." Now it was Mary's turn to struggle to keep her voice steady. "Before you leave tonight, I need to give you something. It's from Beth. It's a letter she was writing to you, and I'm sorry, but I did read it."

My heart leapt up into my throat. I didn't care that Mary had read it, all I cared about was having it. Before I could say anything, the back door opened again and a couple of people came out. Our privacy was gone, and I was going to have to wait until later to find out what Beth wrote.

As I went back into the house, all I could think about was getting that letter. I tried to engage in small talk but fumbled for words and stayed mostly silent. I knew I had to leave soon. I had to know what she had wanted to tell me. Mary caught my eye, and I motioned with my eyes toward the front door. She nodded in understanding and followed me to the spare bedroom, where everyone had left their coats.

I went in first and started to put on my jacket. Mary came in and went to her purse. She pulled out an envelope and handed it to me. We didn't say a word, but we communicated clearly. I slipped the envelope in my inside jacket pocket. I saw her eyes well up. She put her arms around me and hugged me fiercely. We stood embraced in our grief.

I felt her turn her face toward me, and in my ear, she softly said, "She cared for you very much."

My body convulsed and my heart burst out in a single mournful sob. I pressed my face into the nape of her neck as my body shook from the force of my grief. Silently, I wept on her shoulder as she held me close. At that moment, we were the closest connection either of us would ever have to Beth, and we clung to each other, entwined in our sorrow.

I have no idea how long we stayed like that. It seemed like a lifetime; it seemed like a heartbeat. As we separated, we looked knowingly into each other's wet and reddened eyes. I squeezed her hand in farewell and left the room.

I made my round of goodbyes and stepped out into the chilly spring night. I got in my car and started to drive away. A couple of blocks later, I turned onto a side street and pulled over. I removed the envelope from my pocket and turned on the dome light. Hungrily I read her words. Tears began to flow and the words blurred on the pages.

Nancy,

How are you doing, love? Still winter up here and Aspen is crowded with all the spring breakers. So glad I quit the other spa. My new job is so much more relaxed and everyone is so friendly. I must be protected by guardian angels.

Thank you for the lovely letter, it made my day. I love reading your letters. I feel so connected when I read your words. It's as if you are here with me. And I love it! But I'm confused too. Part of me wants to run off and see the world, no ties, no responsibilities. Then I think of you. I feel your hands on me and your breath on my neck as you lean in and I can't imagine my life without you.

I have no idea how it's going to work out between us. You are going back to school and I want to take off and explore the world. But I also want to pursue my dream of creating my own business as I have told you before. So perhaps I should do that while you are in school and then after you graduate we can see where we are. Or maybe I should go explore now, leave you alone while you do law school. Maybe you would study more with me gone!
I'm sorry, love, that I can't commit one way or the other to you. But I do know that I can't imagine my life without you

in it. One thing I do know for certain, you never cease to amaze me.

A primordial howl of anguish erupted from me as I slammed my fist into the dashboard. I had no restraint, and my agony exploded violently out. I wailed and hit anything I could, oblivious to any pain caused to my body. My emotional pain was too great.

"FUCK YOU!" I screamed. "FUCK YOU, FUCK YOU, FUCK YOU, GOD!"

My tears and my rage blinded me, and I flailed about like a madwoman. I felt a depth of anguish I didn't even know could be possible, let alone survive. The only thing I was capable of was rage, and that rage now focused on the only one I believed responsible.

"FUCK YOU, GOD, YOU'RE NOTHING BUT A FUCKING ASSHOLE! HOW DARE YOU CLAIM TO BE LOVING!

"It's just a fucking joke to you. Isn't it?" I whispered painfully. Sobbing I leaned my head back against the headrest. And for a moment, just a moment, I felt at peace, then my rage returned.

"YOU FUCKER!

"I HATE YOU!

"HOW COULD YOU DO THIS? SHE WAS SO KIND, SHE HAD SO MUCH LOVE IN HER, AND YOU JUST SNUFFED IT OUT.

"WHY?

"WHY?

"Why?" I whimpered.

"WHY, GODDAMNIT?!"

I fell back in the driver's seat, exhausted. My attempts to gasp in breath collided with my wails of agony. My tears flowed ceaselessly, and my face and shirt were soaked. Slowly I became aware of my body, and I looked down at my bloody knuckles. Blood smeared on the dashboard, the steering wheel, and the driver's side window. I didn't care. I welcomed the pain. It helped me forget the emptiness, the desolation that now lived inside me.

"I'm done with you," I said. "I will never forgive you, God. You don't care at all. It's just the whims of fate whether we live or die. There is no meaning to our existence. There is no rationality for why one person gets to live, and another dies. There is no higher purpose, no higher justice, no all-encompassing love. It's just a big, fat lie."

I grabbed some napkins out of an old fast-food bag and pressed them to my knuckles. My hands were now starting to swell. I started the car and silently drove home.

※※※※※※※※

"Peace be with you."

Confused, I stared at the man in front of me. I blinked, looked up, and realized suddenly he was reaching out to me for the sign of peace. I had been so absorbed in my thoughts I had lost track of the Mass and where I was. I shook his hand and said, "Peace be with you too." Then I exchanged the gesture with all those around me, as was customary.

The people were now moving forward for the taking of the sacrament. I watched the faithful proceed, their heads bowed. Again, I turned and looked at the confessional.

The couple of years that followed Beth's death were not my finest moments. I lived a hedonistic and amoral lifestyle filled with partying, drugs, alcohol, sex, and cruel indifference to how my actions affected others. I was beyond self-destructive. I was dead, and God help anyone who tried to help or care for me. I hurt my friends and my family as I spiraled into the abyss. I would have perished there if it hadn't been for my mother, whose own near-death experience shook me hard enough to wake me up.

I felt the confessional stare back at me. Forgiveness? Redemption? No, it wasn't for me, not yet. I wasn't ready to forgive myself, and I certainly wasn't ready for absolution, if it was even possible.

It became my row's turn to proceed to the altar. I walked out of the row, but instead of turning right and proceeding up the aisle, I turned left to exit. I pushed the door open and stepped out of the light of the church into the darkness of the night.

DAY TWO

ILLUMINATION

I reached over to the nightstand and looked at my phone. The screen said it was 10:00 a.m. I rolled over, groggy. After I had left the church, I went to a pub close to the hotel and proceeded to do what I always did when I relived that memory; I drank.

Now as I lay in bed with a mild hangover, I attempted to recall what I did. I remembered talking to a pleasant mother and daughter from North Carolina; or was it South Carolina? Whatever, they were fun and chatty. Then I bantered with the bartenders about nothing important. I wanted distractions, shallow conversations, nothing of substance. Nothing that would make me feel. A guy showed up and started to play music and we all listened and sang along. Eventually, the beers and whiskeys hit, and all feelings and memories faded. It was only then that I could go back to my room and fall into oblivion, not haunted by Beth's ghost.

I sighed and got out of bed. I had a lot I wanted to do today. On my list of things to do was to go back to Trinity College and the Book of Kells exhibit. This time I was not going to rush through it like I had when I went two years prior with my parents. After that, I wanted to go to the National Museum of Ireland—Archaeology. Those were my solid plans for the day. If time permitted, I had other sites on my list, but with this late a start, I just didn't know what I was going to get to do.

I got in the shower and felt the water wash away my sins from the night before. I smiled at the thought of going back to the Book of Kells exhibit. I really wanted to absorb it, and the realization that could just take as much time as I wanted was an exhilarating feeling.

Forty minutes later I was out of the hotel, walking up Grafton Street toward Trinity College. The day was again overcast and rainy. Perfect for a day of museums. I reached the end of Grafton, turned right onto Nassau Street and walked down toward the entry closest to Trinity College Library, which housed the Book of Kells exhibit.

The rain had started up and I rushed through the crowded street into the campus and toward the library.

Fortune favored me and I got ahead of a large tour group. I entered the main exhibit area and grabbed an audio guide. I put in the earplugs and tuned everything and everyone else out. This was my time and my personal discovery. I took a deep breath and settled in for an enjoyable and thorough experience, and I was not disappointed. The details in the illustrations around the page borders were fascinating, blending the old Druidic symbolism into the new Christian message.

The Latin words would have been meaningless to the commoner who, illiterate, would have identified with the symbolism on each page. Hidden in all the elaborate knots and lines, the artists skillfully blended the old with the new. The old ways were hidden in plain sight. The Latin text, read by the educated priest, may have been preaching the Jewish faith of the God of Abraham along with the new doctrine of redemption of Jesus Christ, but the old pagan beliefs were also openly represented in those manuscripts.

Humbly, I reflected on the journey of humanity in our quest for expression of thought. Today we text, send pictures, and call each other over vast distances effortlessly. We communicate instantaneously; hell, we send pictures of what we are eating without a second thought. But going through the exhibit, I realized and grasped the effort and significance of what our ancestors went through just to communicate.

Firstly, they had to be literate; they had to be taught to read and write. It was a luxury to indulge in such exercises. Most households fought for survival. They were subject to the fates of a good or bad harvest. It was a grueling existence to provide sustenance. To have the time and money to be taught to read and write was a rare event. It made so much sense to me now why such endeavors were exclusively restricted to the clergy and nobility.

Secondly, there was the whole physicality of writing itself. Back then they wrote on vellum, which was parchment made from the hide of cattle or sheep. This involved butchering, skinning, and tanning. Then there were the acquisitions of the dyes to process the inks for the writing and illustrations of the manuscripts. Some were of local origin, others from distant lands. In short, it was a labor-intensive and expensive ordeal to write.

Thirdly, there was the artistic component. These were illustrated texts filled with symbols and characters of beasts, dragons, and people. So much purpose was employed in the creation of the illustrated manuscripts. The intricacies of the Celtic knots bordering the pages blended the concept of immortality in both a pagan and Christian manner. The serpent swallowing his tail was a holy symbol of reincarnation understood readily by followers of the Druidic religion. The monks who penned these manuscripts understood that they had to communicate the importance of the message of the holy texts regarding reincarnation, immortality, and hope to the people, the overwhelming majority of whom could not read. As such, they knew what symbols to show. It also gave them the opportunity to incorporate two faiths, both speaking the same truth, without incurring the wrath or condemnation of the hierarchy of the Roman Church.

Lastly, despite all these stressors of knowledge, expense, and time associated with producing a written document, men found ways to express their individuality, their humanity, outside of the sanctioned norms of religious or historical texts. Secular poems were expressed, as was the occasional sexual drawing, covertly placed like a hidden gem.

So much of Ireland in the early centuries after the fall of the Roman Empire was dedicated to the preservation of knowledge. As Europe and the Mediterranean fell into disarray with the constant onslaught of invading armies seeking riches, the monks in Ireland built scriptoriums. Here, secluded from the ravages of war, they copied and created these beautiful manuscripts. But Ireland would not remain immune for long, and the Island also would suffer from invasions and destruction.

The Vikings soon discovered the wealth of Ireland and repeatedly raided the island. In fact, the city of Dublin owes its existence to the Norsemen. It wasn't only the Vikings who brought destruction. It was the invasion by Oliver Cromwell that forced the relocation of the Book of Kells to Trinity College for safekeeping. The cycle of creation and destruction seems inherent in humanity's DNA.

I reflected on my own life and realized that perhaps that cycle is hardwired into each of us. We all have such beautiful moments of growth, of creation, and then just as easily we destroy it. Whether it's our careers, our relationships, or our self-worth.

Eventually, I made my way out of the exhibit and into the Long Room of the old library. A cavernous room encased in wood, it always impresses. From the gallery floor, I looked up to another story of stacks of books and above that a curved wood ceiling. It harkened me back to when the institutions of learning were bastions of knowledge and the ability to engage in higher learning was a privilege.

Oh, how I would have loved to be able to get into those stacks and rummage through the books, to finger through the pages of history, to smell the mustiness of the decay of each fragile page. To read the words as if I was a student of another century desperately looking for answers to some question posed by a long-forgotten professor, pondering the information, absorbing its author's thoughts.

Gradually, I made my way out of the library and exited the building. My next stop for the day was the National Museum of Ireland's Archaeology branch. It was around midday, so I figured that I'd find a place to pop in and get some lunch on my way over.

Soon I came up to an establishment and decided to get a bite to eat there.

I sat at a corner table across from the bar and ordered a sandwich and a pint of Guinness. Directly across from me sitting at the bar was an older woman, probably in her late sixties or early seventies. She was alone but kept looking at the door expectantly. She had a pint of Guinness in front of her. From my location, I could indulge in observing her incognito.

First impression; class. Dressed like a country aristocrat in the city for an outing, she wore a traditional soft grey wool sweater with an all-weather hunter-green vest over top. Her hair was tucked up into her tweed wool cap. Her pants were tan. A navy-blue wool overcoat was draped over the back of her chair. On the chair next to her, she had placed her leather purse. As she sat on the bar stool, she held herself with a noble bearing.

Her face looked pensive. She was definitely waiting on someone, but was it joyful or sorrowful? Hard to tell.

She would take sips of her Guinness and then look at the door, then back at the bar in front of her. I ate and watched. Soon I found myself taking a drink when she did. She ordered another pint. By fate, my waitress also stopped by and I ordered another pint. I felt connected to her, like I was looking at myself in the future.

Still, no one arrived. She reached over to her purse in the other chair and eventually pulled out a pack of cigarettes and a lighter. She motioned to the bartender and talked to him briefly. Then she got up and walked out the front door to have a smoke.

I looked at her empty seat, the coat draped over the back of the chair, the purse in the chair next to her. I felt her solitude. I said a silent prayer that her anticipated companion would show up. I knew what she was feeling. I had also wanted, waited, and hoped for someone to show up, or stay in my life. My mind drifted back to Beth and my desire for her to stay with me.

"I thought you were done working in Aspen?" I asked.

"I was. Or at least I thought I was. But the spa called, and they are short a massage therapist for the spring break season." Beth replied.

I rolled over on the bed. I didn't want her to see my tears. But she wasn't fooled. Beth placed her arm across my side and moved her body up close against my back.

"Come on, babe, don't be like this. It's only one more month."

Softly her lips pressed on my neck, but instead of arousing me, it spurred on my sadness.

"I just…" I stammered. "I just was excited to have you back here with me more."

"And I will be. It will go so fast, I'll be back before you know it."

I didn't say anything. My mind was spiraling down a hole of rejection.

"Besides, it's not like I have a job waiting for me down here. This way, I can make some extra money to tide me over while I start to build up a clientele down here." Then in a sheepish voice, Beth added, "Or, you know, figure out my next step."

The sting of her last words brought a fresh wave of tears. It was a dance that was becoming too familiar. Every time I tried to push the relationship forward, Beth side-stepped or avoided talking about it altogether.

"You don't want to move in with me, do you?" I said.

"It's not that I don't want to move in with you. It's just…" Now it was Beth's turn to roll away. "It's just I don't feel ready yet to take that next step."

We laid there with our backs to each other, both of us unsure of whether to take the conversation further. I didn't want to lose her, but I realized I couldn't go on in this state of limbo any longer.

"I love you. I love you so much. But I can't continue on this way. I need to know if you feel the same way. I need to know if you want us to have a future together."

I heard her choke back a sob.

"I love you too."

We both turned to face each other. I reached up and wiped the tears off her cheek.

"I'm not ready to settle down. A part of me just wants to be free. But I don't want it at the expense of you. Nothing makes sense right now," Beth said as she looked into my eyes. "I guess I'm selfish. I want it all and I know that isn't possible."

Why did this have to be so complicated? Why can't being in love be enough? I knew I wanted to wake up every morning for the rest of my life next to her. Why couldn't she feel the same?

"I just need some more time. And being up in Aspen will be good. I'll have the space to get clearer on what I want."

She gently caressed my cheek. "I do love you very much."

I leaned in and brought my lips to her mouth, and as our bodies slowly entwined, I prayed that this was nothing more than a truce and not a stalemate.

⁂⁂⁂⁂⁂⁂⁂⁂

That was the last time we laid together. If I knew of the terrible pain that was lurking before me, would I have acted differently? In the harsh light of 20/20 hindsight. it is so easy to judge one's action. But life doesn't work that way. There are no trial runs, no do overs.

I finished my drink and picked up the tab. It was time to move on to my next destination and to stop dredging up painful memories of the past. I made my way up to the front to pay. At the same time, the woman came back in from smoking and made her way back to her seat. Briefly, we looked at each other and as I looked into her blue eyes I felt like I was looking back into myself. We smiled and passed.

As I was waiting for change, I felt a hand on my shoulder. I turned around and it was her.

"Ye left this on your table," she said in a soft Irish accent.

Confused, I looked down at her hand and saw my phone. Panic briefly gripped my heart as I realized what I had done.

"Oh my God!" I exclaimed. "Thank you so much!"

How could I be so careless? Without my phone, my whole trip would have been turned upside down. Not to mention the vulnerability and isolation I would have felt as my sole lifeline to friends and family would have vanished.

With immense gratitude, I looked at her, but before I could say anything, she softly patted my shoulder, smiled, and teasingly said, "Now ye don't want to be losing this. Ye might miss out on a call from someone special."

Only moments ago, I was wondering if she was waiting on someone, and here she was teasing me on the same subject.

"Well, not much chance of that happening to me," I said jokingly. "I'm here on vacation, and given the distance, anyone I know is still asleep."

"Ah! That's grand." She smiled. "We got some fierce weather for ye." Then, with a wink of her eye and a light squeeze of my arm, "But don't be so sure about that call. Ye never know when it's going to happen."

With that said, she gave me a pat on the shoulder and headed back to her seat. I looked at her walking away, and felt a warmth of friendship, even though I barely knew her. I grabbed my change and headed out the door. It wasn't until I was partway down the street that I realized that she knew I had been at that table. All that time, I thought I had been secretly watching her, given that I was seated behind and off to the side. Now, apparently, she had been aware of me that whole time.

ST. STEPHEN'S GREEN

We finished dinner and I suggested we have dessert on the patio. It was dark, so I lit some candles on the patio table. Dessert was a simple fare of assorted fruits. "Dublin sounds like an interesting city," Jen said. "Funny, I came here wanting to hear about the countryside and the people there. Now I want to know more about Dublin."

"Yes, I love it," I replied.

Jen resumed her place on the patio sofa. I curled up in one of the chairs and stared at the night sky. I smiled at the memory of Dublin. I loved it so much I was contemplating buying a small place there.

"So, what happened after you left that woman?" Jen asked.

"Let's see. After I left the pub, I went to the National Museum of Ireland—Archaeology. And wow! It definitely satisfied the nerd in me. First of all, the building that houses the museum is very old, built in a Victorian-era architectural style, so it was interesting just by itself. Second, it's free!" We both laughed. "You walk into the massive gallery, and it's filled mostly with spectacular gold artifacts. The room is configured so the gold just pops out at you from the lighted display cases. Very dramatic.

"I was enthralled as I moved from exhibit to exhibit. I came to Ireland to learn more about my culture, and I couldn't have picked a better place to get an incredible tutorial. Through the exhibits, I traveled from the Stone Age up to the late Middle Ages. As I looked at the multitudes of gold medallions, collars, jewelry, as well as religious and secular figurines, I saw how skilled the artisans who worked the gold and other metals were. The wealth of ancient Ireland was awe-inspiring.

"I felt really connected to everything there. This was Ireland before the famine, before the tyranny of England's authoritarian policies. This Ireland was a rich and glorious culture of literature, arts, and faith. It was not a nation of paupers.

"Moving through the museum, I felt like an orphan reconnecting with her extended family. To me, it was like listening to family stories. It all meant something on a personal level."

"Cool, but why did you decide to go there in the first place? I mean what was it that drew you to it?" Jen asked.

"You know, I don't really know why. When I was planning what to do in Dublin before I left, it was almost a foregone conclusion that I was going there. In fact, now that I think about it, it was not even an option. I felt driven to go there."

"Well, when I think on it, it kinda makes sense. You wanted to reconnect with your heritage and museums are a good place to start. Of course, they only provide snapshots of one's culture. Did you feel that it helped you?"

"Yes, yes, I do. I saw a beauty and strength in my ancestors I hadn't seen before. I saw myself as a descendant of a rich and vibrant people. Not victims of famine, but rather a people who were resilient, fearless, and powerful. I always felt that, but I didn't know why. Little did I know how much that day was going to be a primer for the rest of my trip."

I looked over and saw the candlelight glow in Jen's eyes. She looked up and saw my gaze. "So, I got you off your story. Please continue."

"I left the museum and was greeted by a lovely autumn evening. The rain had stopped and the clouds had lifted. The sky had a soft glow about it. I walked to the end of the street where it met up with another busy thoroughfare. I looked across and there was St. Stephen's Green.

"I crossed the street and entered the park. The first thing I encountered was a statue in memorial to the famine. The starkness of the figures brought home the essential elements of starvation and hopelessness.

"The park was beautiful. It was an oasis in the concrete, urban sprawl that surrounded it. The tranquility that I felt was intoxicating. I strolled down the path and looked at the various people walking about. The leaves were starting to change, and many had already fallen to the ground.

"There's a lake in the center of the park full of ducks, seagulls, and swans. The walkways traverse the circumference of the park and the lake. There are numerous side paths to take, and huge trees canvas the area. If I lived in Dublin, this would definitely be a habitual walking area."

"Sounds so lovely," Jen said. "It seems that no matter how much we remove the grass and the trees to put up our buildings and roads, we still long to connect back to the earth."

"Yes, I agree." I smiled and felt at peace.

"It had a homely feel about it. I have never seen myself as a huge city person. I never had the desire to live in New York City, Chicago, or Los Angeles, but as I strolled through that park, I began to consider living in Dublin, at least part-time."

What I didn't say to Jen was that while I was in the park, a seed of doubt had been planted. A deceptive thought of comfort was taking root.

After I left the park, I went and got dinner. As I sipped on my beer, I started to seriously think about not leaving Dublin at all. It was my last night in Dublin until I flew out.

The next day, I planned to trek out on the unscripted part of my adventure. The part with no safety net. But here in the comfort of the pub, I started to consider canceling my plans to go out and explore the southeast area of Ireland. It was a seductive thought. I was now familiar with Dublin. I felt safe. And for Christ's sake, a hurricane was bearing down on the island.

I rationalized to myself about how much more there was to see in the city. How I could explore the gay scene, maybe even meet some people here. I had a nice hotel to stay in. It felt so right and so logical. Why leave this vibrant city and go out alone into the unknown? Maybe Julie was right. Maybe it was a stupid idea to do this trip, to be alone, far from anyone who knows me. Far from anyone who cares about me

I felt out of my depth. Who was I kidding? I wasn't any great adventurer, and I certainly wasn't any hip, dynamic woman. I was just me. Someone whose attempts to reach for more from life had been consistently met with disappointment and rejection. Life had beaten me down and put me in my place.

What was I doing here? Why did I constantly think I was something more than what I actually was? I was pathetically looking for someone who lived a lifetime ago. Before a multitude of bad decisions. Who I was, or better yet, who I thought I was, existed only in my memories now. I had lost her.

I looked up from my beer and stared across the room to the bar in front of me. I saw my reflection in the mirror behind the bar, and what I saw disturbed me greatly. Looking back at me was a sad and lonely middle-aged woman, her best years behind her. Invisible to the laughing crowd around her. Disappearing in plain sight.

I had a choice to make. I looked at the glass in my hands. I felt small, and honestly, I felt afraid of both choices before me. My eyes lifted back to look at the woman in the mirror. It was then that I knew.

No, I would not stay in Dublin. I didn't come here to play it safe. I came here to find that lost woman. I came here to be brought back to life.

DAY THREE

THE GARDEN

Sleepily, I rolled over and looked over toward the window. Through the sheer drapes, I could see it was a bright and sunny day. I sighed and swung myself upright. An hour later I was in a cab heading over to the car rental. It wasn't a super early start, but early enough for what I had planned for the day.

Within fifteen minutes, I had my keys and a map out of Dublin.

I got in on the right side of the car and oriented myself to driving once again on the left side of the road. As my phone was connecting to the car's Bluetooth system, I looked over the map again that would take me to the N11 road and out of Dublin toward Powerscourt.

I was excited about this next phase of the trip. I couldn't believe that twelve hours ago I was so willing to chuck it all and stay put.

"All right, girlie, let's blow this town," I said to myself.

I made two lefts, which put me on a busy three-lane street. Confidently, I drove.

I drove parallel to the Grand Canal. I looked out at a beautiful residential area. Small restaurant barges floated peacefully at their moorings. People jogged or walked alongside the canal, some with their dogs. I fantasized about finding a place in this area. A small flat in one of the townhouses that lined the road. I could pop in and out of town. Become a regular. Know the local haunts, where to go for coffee, eclectic little bistros for lunch, a fun pub to drop in and share the craic.

The traffic was heavy, and I still didn't see a major intersection, nor did I see any signs for the N11. As I kept traveling down the road, the area became less residential, and I saw more professional offices and businesses. I approached the Grand Canal Dock and had to accept the fact that I had missed the turn and now was lost.

I found a place to pull over and got my phone out. I looked up the address for Powerscourt House and put it into my GPS.

I should have done this in the beginning, I said angrily.

I confidently started back in the direction I had just come from. Traffic was very heavy and changing lanes was difficult.

A soothing voice emanated from my GPS. "In 400 meters, make a left onto Sussex Road."

"What?"

I had no idea how far 400 meters was.

"Is it far?"

Deaf to my inquiries, the voice chimed, "In 200 meters, make a left onto Sussex Road."

Crap! I needed to get over, and quickly. Desperately, I made my way across the lanes, driving quickly in order to shoot in the gaps. I accelerated and squeezed into the far-left lane, embarrassed at how closely I cut in.

"Turn left."

Shit! The road was immediately before me. With no time to signal, I hit the brakes and turned way too fast onto the road. I didn't look into my rearview mirror, but I could envision the hand gesture and the string of expletives that I'm sure were sent in my direction. For the next mile, I didn't look to either side of me, afraid of the angry faces I would meet. I openly confessed my driving sin to God and asked for forgiveness.

My act of contrition must have been accepted because the rest of the journey out of Dublin was uneventful. Once on the N11, I relaxed and briefly celebrated that I had made it out of the city. I laughed at my hubris in thinking I didn't need to use my GPS. Lord, what was I thinking?

In a very short time, I made it to Powerscourt, my first destination for the day. Established in the 1700s, it was a former private estate of the Viscounts Powerscourt. In 1961, it was sold to a private owner, but in 1974 the house was destroyed by fire. Today it stood only partially renovated. However, it wasn't the house that I came here for, it was the gardens. I paid my entry fee and proceeded out the doors to a breathtaking first view.

I looked on with amazement at this part of the estate, called the Italian Garden. Impressive stone terraces provided a dramatic overlook of the estate with Sugarloaf Mountain in the background. Pebble mosaic stairs led down through groomed lawns and onto the perron, an Italianate stairway, toward a lake situated directly ahead guarded by two statues of Pegasus atop a stone boathouse. In the middle of the lake was a huge fountain shaped in the image of Triton.

I walked directly down the middle of the perron, eyes fixed on Triton. I wanted to feel powerful. Everything about this garden was designed with a purpose: to inspire or intimidate; to embolden or humble; to enlighten or mystify. Slowly, I descended to the lake.

People who were going back up toward the house moved to one side or the other. No one challenged my position. It was like a parting of the waters. Is this what power is? Nothing more than the act of taking it, knowing most of us are unwilling to challenge?

How many times have I just given away my power?

I stopped on the last landing before reaching the lake. As I looked out upon Triton spewing water up toward the heavens, I realized it was too many times to count.

I'd given it to my lovers, my enemies, my friends, and my family. Sometimes I fought for my power, but most times it was passively acquiesced. Once given, it was next to impossible to reclaim. The enemy who demeaned you, the friend who disrespected you, the lover who betrayed you, all held dominion. The dynamics were set. To regain parity would be a constant struggle. Like two stags, you lock horns, each trying to push the other back, to gain ground, to get control.

I looked out at the lake. In Greek mythology, Triton was the herald, a messenger, for his father, Poseidon. Was it his call that had summoned me to cross the ocean and return to my ancient homeland?

The only thing I knew for certain was that I took this trip because I was uncertain who I was anymore. I needed to reclaim my power. Now that I was here, I felt my self-doubts resurface and take hold.

I stopped at the railing on top of the boathouse and looked out on the lake. I closed my eyes and felt the heat of the sun and the mist of water from the fountain. I heard muted voices and footsteps upon the paths, the wind through the trees, and the distant songs of birds.

I sighed. Such deep thoughts for a lovely day.

I opened my eyes and turned to set off on the path around the right side of the lake. The landscape changed from the vast open lawns of the Italian garden, and I found myself on a narrow pathway through heavy vegetation, with trees canopied overhead, and grasses and flowering shrubs lining the pathway around the lake.

This was a place for lovers. The intimacy of the space and the softness of the flora all stirred up the romantic in me. I wished I had a lover's hand to hold. Beth's hand. For a brief moment, as I gazed up at the canopy, I thought that I could feel her hand in mine. But when I looked down all I saw was the emptiness of my open hand turned to the sky.

Not willing to leave her ghost behind, I walked along the winding path, remembering the feel of her arms around me as she pressed her body against mine, the breeze soft like her fingertips upon my skin, and the sun on my face like the heat of her lips upon mine.

I smiled at the memories as I walked the path to the other end of the lake. Strange, after all this time, that I should be thinking about her so much. Unexpectedly, she was here with me on this trip. The night in the church, the next day in pub, and now here in this serene garden, her presence forced itself upon me. Time was irrelevant. I still missed her as if she had passed yesterday, not twenty-plus years ago. The truth is, love exists outside the construct of time. It has no beginning or end; it always was and will always be.

At the other end of the lake, the path branched off in multiple directions. I went off to the right and the path led me into a forest of giants. I looked upon them with awe and marveled at each tree's immense presence. For centuries they had stood here as sentinels, impervious to all who gazed upon them. The birds nested up in their boughs, while lovers embraced under the shade. Old men rested upon the trunks and reflected on their lives. Widows sat and remembered when they were young. Yet nothing mattered to these giants but the path of the sun as the earth turned on its axis.

I walked aimlessly, lost in the flow of my thoughts. Eventually, the path turned and went downhill into thicker vegetation. Now the sun struggled to reach the forest floor, and the area was cast in shadow by the tall oaks, firs, and other trees. The light off the green leaves of the rhododendrons, ferns, and elephant ears cast a mystical green glow. I stopped and looked around, confused.

I'm lost, I muttered to myself as I looked down at the map.

I thought I was heading to the dolphin fountain and instead I was in this thick, jungle-like area. The worst part was I had no idea how I got here. I just walked without thinking and now I was here, wherever that was, and no one else was around.

I had two options before me. One was to turn around, go back up the hill and try and figure out where I missed the path to the fountain. The other was to keep going in the same direction and see where it would take me.

As I stood pondering my next move, I felt a presence flood into my mind, a woman's soft, lilting Irish voice, similar to the one I thought I had heard in the bathtub. I froze.

> *In the silence, you stand not knowing what to do.*
> *Maybe nothing?*
> *Maybe you should run?*

But where? Back up the hill,
or into the void?
Doesn't matter.

Just run, that's what you want to do,
it's what you always do.
But all decisions have consequences,
as well you know.

"Whoa! What was that all about?" I said out loud.

Like the other night, I looked around to see who was here with me. No one. It was just me standing alone on the path. The overgrowth of plants suddenly felt claustrophobic. My heart raced. I wanted to run. Run out of here, away from whatever had just happened.

I looked at the hill I had just come down. It was the surest way out. I looked at the path ahead of me. It narrowed and descended further into the forest. As I looked, I knew. It was more a feeling than a thought.

Still shaken by whatever had just transpired, I walked on into the forest. No sound came from my footfalls as they landed upon the soft carpet of leaves and pine needles. The forest growth thickened and formed a tunnel as I made my way along the path.

Part of me wanted to run back up that hill. But I didn't. Instead, I stepped further into the darkness of the forest. It felt familiar, like it knew me. I don't know why I thought this, but one thing I was certain of, it knew that I needed to go into the dark. I needed to remember.

Gone now were the soft memories of Beth. In their stead was Brynn and the harshness of that reality. I went forward on the forest path back into a past I had come to escape from.

⁂⁂⁂⁂⁂⁂⁂⁂

Sitting in my house in Colorado I listened to the ringtones. "Come on, pick up," I whispered into the phone.

"Hello?"

"Hey! Brynn, I got some great news. I decided to take the position in Santa Fe. I'm going to be moving there! I blurted out."

"That's great! Oh, I'm so excited to have you here. Congratulations!"

"I am too. This is going to be so great. I can't wait to spend more time with you."

Ever since that night in Santa Fe, we stayed in touch. We talked on the phone and shared deep conversations about love, relationships, and spirituality. A couple of weeks later, I made a quick trip to Denver and had dinner with her and some mutual acquaintances, including Maren. That night, as we said our goodnights, she hugged me and then briefly, but passionately, pressed her lips on mine. It was done quickly and discreetly, so as not to arouse the attention of the others. But its effect was mind-blowing.

For me, the dynamics of what was transpiring that night were far from clear. Although I knew Brynn's marriage was falling apart and my relationship with Maren was in its death throes, I still was unsure. But with each interaction, I was more and more certain of who I wanted to be with. Brynn. Now, months later, it seemed that my fantasy of being able to be near Brynn was becoming a reality.

"I'm coming into town next week to finalize everything and to look for a place to rent."

"Okay. Do you want to stay with me?"

Yes, yes, I did. Very much.

"Yeah, that would be great. But only if it's okay with you."

"Absolutely! Oh, this is so exciting!"

I was set to arrive on a Sunday. On Monday I would meet with the owners of the barn I was going to work out of to finalize the payment arrangements and other logistics. It wasn't an ideal arrangement, but it did get me back into a situation through which I could rebuild my business to be similar to what I had in Florida. More importantly, it got me closer to Brynn.

Late Sunday, I drove into town and to Brynn's house. I was tired but excited. And nervous. Since that night in Denver, we had never spoken of that kiss. Did it mean what I thought? Maybe I read too much into it? For hours, self-doubt ran rampant in my mind as I drove along the desolate highways toward Santa Fe.

We ate and talked about everything that was happening, everything except the possibility of us. After dinner, we sat on the couch sipping tequila. The closeness of her body intoxicated me far more than the alcohol. After a rough two years separating from my ex-wife, and the ups and downs of Maren, I felt hopeful.

The night was getting late, and we could no longer avoid the subject of where I was going to sleep.

Brynn took the empty glass from my hand and looked at me intently. "You have two choices tonight of where to sleep. I can get some blankets and you can sleep on the couch or…" there was a pause and her voice softened, "you can sleep in my bed."

I felt so shy and insecure. I dropped my eyes, afraid that they would betray me and tell her all my secrets. Of my longing and desire to be more than just her friend, that she rocked my world, and my fear that she would see all that and recoil from me.

With what I hoped sounded cool and controlled I said, "Well, I think the bed would be much more comfortable."

And so, platonically, we lay together. We talked briefly some more, and then she drifted off to sleep, but I just lay there, staring out the window at the night sky, with her so close and yet so far. I felt her warmth, I felt the slight rise and fall of the bed with her breath. I could smell her hair, the fragrance of her skin. It wouldn't take much, just a shift of my body, one way or the other, and a decision would be made.

But I did neither. I just lay there, lost. Everything was still, and in the darkness, I listened to her sleep.

The next morning, I felt her shift in the bed. As I drifted between sleep and wakefulness, I thought I felt her lips softly on my cheek. Was this a dream? I felt my heart stop, frozen with fear. Before I could fully register what had just happened, I felt her fingertips softly caress the side of my face.

Startled, I jerked my body and I opened my eyes. I looked up at her and knew this was not a dream. It was real. And I was terrified.

"Good morning," she said, smiling down at me. "How did you sleep?"

I swallowed hard and tried to compose myself.

"Good," I croaked out.

With a smile, she swung out of bed and headed to the bathroom. I lay frozen. How could I bungle this so badly? Why was I so terrified? I had fantasized about this moment so many times, and now that it was here, I was catatonic. I heard her come out of the bathroom.

"I'm going to make some coffee."

She went down the stairs, and I forced myself to get up. I got in the shower and started to wake up. So many things on my mind: the new job, moving, leaving the few customers I had in Colorado, and her. I had no idea how I was going to make it all work. It all seemed beyond my abilities. I fought the urge to run out of there.

I'm not handling this very well, I thought.

Minutes later, I was dressed, my bag by the front door, and a cup of coffee in my hand.

We shared our mundane details for the day. No mention of last night or this morning. Each of us skirted around the elephant in the room. Eventually, it was time for me to go. As we hugged goodbye, I held her close and felt a force within me telling me to kiss her. To let her know how I really felt. But my fear was stronger as it forcefully reminded me of the pain of feeling that much for a person and the devastation when they went away. I disentangled myself. We looked at each other, the loss of the moment unspoken between us.

It took me a month to settle everything. I found a place to live, got my house rented, and gave my customers time to make arrangements. During this time, I had loosely kept in touch with Brynn. I was afraid that I would scare her off if I called too much. I rationalized that it was better if I got settled in, and then I would let her know how I truly felt. Yes, that was a safe, sane, and rational plan.

I was so insecure. She and her friends were so sophisticated, so hip, I didn't want to appear to be the geek that I really was. And no matter how desperately I wanted to be brave and tell her about my true feelings for her, my heart recoiled in terror at the possibility of opening up.

෴෴෴෴෴෴෴

The Irish sun blinded me as I emerged from the thick forest. Blinking rapidly, my eyes adjusted to the light, and I looked out at Sugarloaf Mountain. I could tell that I was now at the edge of the estate. The fencing that separated the estate from the next property was simply made of wire. I was definitely away from the main tourist part of the gardens. The bramble grew thickly along it and, in some places, overtook the wire, encasing it. I was surrounded by silence.

Here I was, thousands of miles from Santa Fe and years removed from this episode in my life, and yet it still hurt to recall it. I looked at the path; it was just a grassy space between the trees. Few people ventured out here. I looked back at where I had just come from. The path disappeared into the darkness of the forest. I looked back at the mountain and the dark clouds above it. I turned and looked at the path leading back to the main part of the estate and how it gradually lost its grassy, wild nature. I looked at my feet. I didn't move. A force inside me held me transfixed here. I wasn't done yet. The forest knew there was still more to remember, more uncomfortable truths to confront.

A few days before I was sent to move, I called Brynn.

"Hey, I'm almost all packed up and will be in town this Saturday."

"That's wonderful. Just let me know. Hope it all goes smoothly."

"Me too. I have a good friend helping me, but it's still a daunting task."

Silence on the line. My nerves started to act up. Quickly I started talking about the logistics of the move. But something was wrong.

Brynn broke in on my inane diatribe. "I need to tell you something before you get down here. You see, I don't want there to be any mixed messages and it's best to just be upfront."

Silence.

"I've started dating someone. So, I just don't want you to think there's going to be anything other than friendship between us."

Silence.

"And, well, I don't mix friendship and lovers. I don't like it messy like that. So, I just want to be clear that we are just friends."

Silence.

"I think that's really all you want, anyway."

Silence.

I then said the most dishonest thing I had ever uttered.

"Yeah, no problem. I'm fine with us just being friends."

I hung up. Tears welled in my eyes. Everything was closing in on me, crushing my chest. I couldn't breathe and my head was spinning. My world tilted on its axis and contracted.

I stared at the boxes ready to be loaded, then out the window at my dog lying contently in the grass. Everything was just as it had been before the call, yet everything had changed.

Then I had the most dishonest thought.

I'm going to fix this. I'm going to get her back.

WATERFALL

I paused in my story and took a sip from my drink. Jen sat silently, absorbing what I had just shared. The stillness of the night felt suffocating.

"I know it seems strange that I went to Ireland to rediscover myself and here I am telling you all my history," I said finally.

Jen took a sip from her drink. "No, not really," she said.

She looked at her glass and continued, "I think we often go on adventures, or journeys, or some form of sabbatical, thinking that we will find the solution out there. A desire for something that will make us whole. A cure that exists outside of us. It is waiting for us in some destination or person. In reality, all we do is carry our baggage with us. I'm curious, did you consciously bring up these memories or do you think it was spontaneous and subconscious?"

"I don't think so."

Jen stared at me.

"I mean not consciously."

Jen still stared at me.

"Um, well…maybe?"

Jen smiled at me. "Perhaps the answer isn't so black and white. I think we often lie to ourselves about our intentions. Not purposefully, but sometimes we protect ourselves from the unpleasant realities of our lives."

I thought about that for a minute before I answered.

"I went to Ireland with the intention to escape. Of leaving everything behind. Honestly, I wanted to reinvent myself. I wanted to be someone different than who I was. What I didn't count on was the resurfacing of these old scars."

I looked into my glass. What I was about to reveal still hurt, and I still couldn't discuss it comfortably. But I knew I needed to say it.

"What I left out about that night with Brynn, the reason why I was frozen, had a history that even now I struggle with. As I mentioned before, Rachael and I had issues and one of the big ones revolved around sex and intimacy. The angrier Rachael became in the relationship the more she used sex as a weapon. Lovemaking became torturous as she took pleasure in criticism and denial of satisfaction. Simple acts of intimacy on my part such as hugging were either pushed off as unwanted or twisted as somehow coercive on my part. By the end, I was so upside down that I avoided any overt acts of affection for fear of the repercussions. Any confidence that I had that someone was interested in me was gone."

The night was silent as Jen absorbed what I had just revealed.

"I was riddled with so much self-doubt after Rachael that I didn't trust my instincts. I didn't trust that what I was feeling would be reciprocated, that it would be wanted."

"I'm so sorry, Nancy. I'm at a loss for words right now."

I wiped a tear from my eye. It still hurt and every time I thought about this it felt like I was picking open an old wound so it could bleed all over me again. I took a deep breath and smiled at Jen.

"Well, enough of that. Let's get back to the story." I said as an end of discussion on this matter.

Jen smiled back understandingly.

"So, what did you do next?" she asked.

"I finished the rest of my tour of the estate and had a late lunch. I had spent way more time than I thought I would and realized that I wasn't going to get in as much as I had planned for the day.

"But I really wanted to see the Powerscourt Waterfall. There was a section of land between the estate and the waterfall that was under different ownership, so that meant I had to leave the estate and drive to it. After lunch, I got back in the car and entered the address in my GPS. I made my way pretty quickly to the site. Again, I wasn't disappointed.

"The waterfall is on the River Dargle and is almost a 400-foot drop. I went down to the bottom and stood transfixed as massive amounts of water constantly cascaded from such heights. The only sounds were the roar and rush of the water as it came off the rocks and fell into the pool at the base. Then the water flowed down through the surrounding forest on its way to the sea.

"Once again, I was alone. The few other tourists that were around didn't venture past the main viewing area. I scrambled down to the river, which was the size of a mountain stream, and hopped from boulder to boulder until I was in the middle, looking back up through the conifer trees to the waterfall. The mist of the water softly enveloped me. The water flowing at my feet gurgled and giggled as it slipped over the rocks."

What I didn't know how to tell Jen, without sounding insane, was all the intense sensations I felt as I stood there, eyes closed. I heard the wind through the pine boughs, the water as it fell into the pool, the snap of a twig, the chirps and tweets of the birds. I felt the coolness of the air and the mist on my face. I smelled the musty dampness of the soil and the wet bark of the trees.

My soul leapt up in joy and danced upon the droplets. My heart burst out in a song matched only by the chorus of the birds above me. A peacefulness swept over me and I longed to stay here, become old with the stones, and live serenely through the seasons with only the movement of water as it transmuted from raging torrent to mist and eventually settled into the soft flow of the stream.

Instead, I cut to the part where I was ready to leave this magical place.

"So, I soon realized that the shadows were growing long and I needed to leave and continue on my journey. Once back in my car I looked up the location for my next scheduled stop, Glendalough and St. Kevin's monastery.

"I picked up my phone and went to enter the destination, but something was wrong. No cell service. After I got over the initial shock, I shrugged it off. No problem, I'd just do it the old-fashioned way. I rummaged in my bag and pulled out a road atlas. After a few minutes I had the route planned and I started out of the park."

"Good for you!" Jen said. "It's crazy how dependent we have become on technology. I love that you just whipped out the map and kept going."

I laughed. "Well, it didn't go that smoothly. I drove out confidently and it was just a couple of turns until I would be on the main road to take me to Glendalough. I zipped past a couple of small side roads, but there was no signage, so I wasn't concerned that they were anything I needed to worry about.

"As I drove, I kept thinking I would be coming up on one of my turns soon, but the road just kept going with no hint of an intersection. Just like earlier in the day as I was attempting to leave Dublin, I began to get the sinking feeling that I was going in the wrong direction. I looked at my phone and it still didn't register any connection. Now I definitely had the feeling I was going in the wrong direction, but I had no way of knowing which way that was.

"I kept looking down at my phone, hoping that at one of the hilltops I would finally get cell service. The road dipped and twisted down through a pretty little glen. The hillsides were open grazing fields bordered by heather and other shrubs. At the bottom, the road crossed over a little stream and then started back up. At the top of the hill, I looked at my phone quickly and to my immense relief, I saw that I had service, albeit a weak one.

"Up ahead the road widened out and I pulled over onto the shoulder. It was sunny so I put down the windows for some air while I worked on getting my GPS up and running. As I stared at my phone, inputting the address for Glendalough, I had the feeling that I was being watched.

"I looked up and out the windshield. There was nobody around; not even a car had passed me. I continued on with getting my route entered in, but I still felt like I was being watched.

"I looked up again. Nothing. I looked back down again at my phone. Yet I couldn't shake the feeling. The hairs on the back of my neck tingled and every instinct told me I wasn't alone. Then finally, the route came up on my phone."

"BAAAAAA!"

As if I had been electrocuted, I jumped up in my seat. The phone flew out of my hand.

"JESUS FUCKING CHRIST!" I yelled.

Quickly, I turned my head toward the passenger seat and was met by the imperious stare of a ram.

"'BAAAAAA!' He screamed at me again through the window.

"I could still feel the shock of that encounter. How my heart was pounding, my breathing hard. My hands started to shake as the adrenaline from the fright shot through my body."

Jen burst out laughing. "Oh my God!"

"I know, right? He scared the shit out of me," I said, laughing.

"What happened next?"

"We just stared at each other. He looked at me with the disdain one feels when some door-to-door solicitor comes unannounced to the house peddling his wares. Numb with shock, I stared back into his black face, unsure of what I should do or say next.

"I guess he decided I was a complete idiot and not worth his attention. Eventually, he moved away from the car and back into the field. By now the shock had worn off and I started to laugh. All I could think was, *Oh my God! Did that really just happen?*

"I looked around the car and eventually found my phone wedged down the side of the driver's seat. I retrieved my route and sure enough, my suspicions were confirmed. I had been driving in the opposite direction.

"My course laid in, and seemingly all systems operational, I started to turn the car out onto the road. But before I did, I looked one last time over at the ram. He was now peacefully eating with the other sheep and seemed to give me no further attention.

"I don't know why, but I called out of the window to him.

"'Bye, buddy.'

"He lifted his head and looked at me. Then I swear he shook his head as if I was the stupidest person he had ever met."

GLENDALOUGH

S lightly out of my comfort zone, I pushed on the accelerator to make up for lost time. The car bounced on the narrow road. I was nowhere close to my planned schedule for the day. Having accepted defeat, my hope at this stage was to make it to Glendalough and St. Kevin's monastic site before nightfall. As I pulled into the parking lot of St. Kevin's, a sign said the site closed at five. I looked at my phone. It was ten minutes to five.

I parked the car and decided to just pop in to make arrangements to come visit in the morning and ask them where a good place to stay would be.

Two women were behind the counter in the main reception area. They looked at me as I approached.

"We close at five," one of the women said.

"Yes, I know."

"Are you going to look around the place?" she asked.

"Well, I don't know. It's only ten minutes and I don't really want to pay for it," I replied.

The lady smiled. "You don't need to pay to just go walk around. It's only to see the exhibits in the visitor's center that you need to pay for."

I looked at them, shocked. I never thought that I could go into a park or exhibit like this and not pay.

She continued, "In fact, you should go look around tonight, because we have that storm coming in and it will be a horrible day tomorrow. So why don't you go wander around? It's totally open."

"I will, thanks. By the way, where is a good place to stay?"

"Did you come up through Laragh?" she asked.

"Yes, I believe I did."

I didn't think much of the town as I was driving through, except for a wonderful smoky smell that came out of a restaurant. *I'm definitely going to eat dinner there tonight*, I thought as I drove past.

"That's where you want to stay," she exclaimed. Her co-worker nodded in agreement.

"You don't want to stay up here in the big fancy hotel. Laragh is a great place, with good food and much more reasonable lodging. Very nice bed and breakfast places." She turned to her co-worker for confirmation.

"Oh yes, much nicer," the other lady chimed in.

I thanked them and left. There were many reasons I wanted to visit this place: the historical nature of the site, the beautiful scenery, and St. Kevin, known as the St. Francis of Ireland. Before he founded the monastery, he lived as a hermit in a cave above Glendalough Upper Lake and was known for his ability to communicate with animals. As with so many of the early followers of Christianity, there appeared to be a blend of the pagan ways and beliefs with the new Christian religion. It was a symbiosis that I felt drawn to.

I started down the pathway to the entrance. I looked off to my right and saw the outside patio of the Glendalough Hotel. To me, the hotel was a large and somewhat obtrusive structure, but there was no denying it had a prime location. Well, if I couldn't find anything down in Laragh, this would not be a bad place to stay. I could tell it would stretch my budget, but I had planned accordingly.

I walked through the remains of a double-stone archway. The sky was starting to change, giving it a magical glow. As I walked through the archway, I felt an energy shift as if I had crossed through a portal.

I emerged out the other side surrounded by mountains, woodlands, and a meadow. A stream ran down from the mountains through the meadow. It was a place left behind by time. Here there were no such things as cars, airplanes, the Internet, or anything of the modern world. It was just still. The only sounds were the birds singing of their day and the wind coming down through the trees.

There were still a few people milling about, but everyone respected the solitude and serenity of this place. I knew that this was a very popular tourist destination and had expected it to have a cold commercialized feel about it. But I was wrong. Instead, I felt a calmness I hadn't experienced in a long time. I couldn't remember when I last felt this. I began to realize that getting lost hadn't been solely an exercise in frustration. There was a deeper purpose. Fate had brought me here at this late hour so that I could feel the magic.

From this ancient place founded in the sixth century, there remained a round tower and multiple buildings, including an intact church from the twelfth century known as St. Kevin's Kitchen. As I walked around, I noticed gravestones everywhere. Some were standing, some were lying down. Some you could read. Others were lost to the corrosion of time. A robin perched on one, curiously watched me as I wandered through the graveyard. Amazingly, I saw that people had been buried there as late as the 1970s. Ireland, I mused, so much of its past was visible, tangible, just as obvious and prevalent as the trappings of the asphalt roads, cell towers, and steel structures of modern society.

Eventually, the path led me away from the buildings to a bridge over the stream. I crossed over and entered a forest. It was old, still, and dark. The forest floor was bare, with only a few ferns and trunks covered in emerald moss. This was an ancient place left alone from the ravages of industry for centuries. To me, it felt as if I had yet again stepped into another world.

For the third time that day, I left the crowds behind and wandered off in solitude among the trees. This time I did so purposefully. Would that voice find me here? Was it just a fluke or a figment of my imagination? And honestly, I didn't know if I would welcome it or be scared out of my mind.

Slowly, I walked the path among the trees. Unlike the episode at Powerscourt, here I felt hidden and safe, as if I had entered a sanctuary. I wish I had planned on spending a full day here, but I hadn't expected to be so enchanted. In fact, my original thought was to quickly see Powerscourt, swing up here to Glendalough to visit the ruins, and then head on toward the coast to stay for the night. I chuckled to myself as it was clearly apparent that the day had not gone at all as planned.

Twilight fell when I emerged from the forest and came to a second bridge to cross back over the water. Midway, I stopped and leaned on the wood railing. I looked up the stream across the meadow to the round tower in the distance; the mountains shadowed in the backdrop. It was surreal. The air was pleasant and comforting. I closed my eyes, and all I could hear was the running of the water over the stones. I stood transfixed, absorbing all the magic that was here. I was nowhere and everywhere. I was past and I was present.

There was a shift of air and I sensed that I was no longer alone. I opened my eyes and looked at a blackbird perched on the railing. He cocked his head and looked imperiously at me.

"Well, hello there, little fellow," I said softly.

He let out a quick and short lilt of a song in acknowledgment of my greeting.

After the day's events, I stopped questioning the improbable. Was it any more fanciful to believe a bird just answered me or that some supernatural force was talking to me in my head?

The rational explanation was the same for both: I was nuts.

But I didn't feel crazy. Quite the opposite. I felt more sane than I had in a long time, standing here conversing with my feathered friend.

"You are probably wondering why I'm here," I said. "Well, partly it's to pay homage to your patron saint. Oh yes, he's famous. Well at least in Ireland and with Catholics."

We both looked back up toward the tower.

"But that's not the only reason. You see, I'm lost. I've lost myself. Maybe being here I'll find my way again. A long time ago, my ancestors lived here. I guess I'm hoping by coming back I too will find my roots, my foundation. Because honestly, my friend, I need to believe there is more. That there is more to this existence than what I've been living."

I looked over and saw that he had not flown off.

"So, my little friend, how about you? Why are you sitting here listening to some mad American woman? Maybe you can help me out? Tell me about your ancient ways. Lead me to hidden sanctuaries where I can lie down and be reborn. Or perhaps you would be so kind as to send a guide for me."

He looked one last time at me before he raised his head up to the heavens and sang a song. His notes, shrill, pure, and true, floated in the air, dipped over the water, and rang out across the meadow before rising over the trees and dissolving into the night sky.

LARAGH

The sun shed its last light as I drove into Laragh. I saw lots of signs for B&Bs, but all of them said *No Vacancy*. It wasn't looking good. I chastised myself for spending so much time up at St. Kevin's and not being responsible about finding a place to stay for the night. Yet a part of me wouldn't have given up anything I had just experienced.

"It's not going to be pretty; it's not going to be quaint, but I see a hotel and I'm going to stop there," I said to myself.

I walked into the lobby. Nobody was around and the place looked deserted. I rang the bell and waited. There was a pub off to the left side of the lobby. I rang the bell again.

"Well, it's definitely off-season," I muttered.

I rang the bell a third time and wondered whether I should go into the pub and ask if anybody was around to check me in. Suddenly a lady popped her head out from around a wall behind the reception desk. I jumped back, startled.

"I thought I heard somebody," she said.

"Yes," I said nervously, still a bit shaken by her sudden appearance. "I'm looking for a room for the night."

"I'm closed for the season. I'm doing repairs. I don't have any room that's available for you," she said hurriedly.

My heart sank. Was this going to be the night I slept in my car? I felt a mild panic rise. I closed my eyes and took a deep breath. *It is what it is*, I told myself. I resigned myself to going back up to the hotel in Glendalough and seeing how expensive it was going to be. I turned to go back out.

"Wait, wait, wait," she said softly. "I have some friends who have B&Bs close by. They're just down the road." She gestured in the direction of the door.

"They're right next to each other, go try them. Tell them I sent you, that I don't have any rooms. We all help each other out here. I know they will help you."

I thanked her as she gave me the names of two places. I went to the first one, but it was all booked up. The next B&B she mentioned was literally next door. I pulled in.

I knocked on the door and a woman appeared.

"Hello, I'm sorry to bother you so late, but I'm looking for a room for the night and the lady at the hotel said I should ask you," I said.

Perhaps it was the forlorn look on my face, but her eyes looked on me with a kindness born from seeing more than one travel orphan on her doorstep seeking shelter for the night. Deirdre, as I later learned her name, looked behind me and saw I was traveling alone.

"Come in," she said as she pulled the door fully open. "I got one room left. If you like it, it will be fifty euros for the night."

I entered and followed her to the room. The house was very lovely, and the room was spacious with a double bed, a sitting area and a private bathroom. It more than met my expectations. I agreed to take the room and she handed me the set of keys, one for the room and the other for the front door.

"Now, you can come and go as you please, just make sure the door is locked," she said. "Breakfast starts at seven and there is always tea and coffee available in the breakfast room."

"Thank you so much. I really appreciate it," I said.

"Now you are going to want to get something to eat and to listen to some music."

"Well, yes, actually that's exactly what I want to do."

"The hotel where you came from has a very good restaurant and a very good pub. And they have live music. There is usually some guy in the corner with a guitar."

"That sounds perfect for tonight," I said.

It was so close I could have walked there. In fact, she suggested that I do that.

"There's a walking path to the hotel. You just have to cross the road and go through the gate. It's walled off, so you don't have to worry about traffic."

"Actually, I passed a restaurant earlier that had this wonderful wood smoke coming out of it, and I thought I'd go there tonight," I said.

She smiled. "Oh yes, it's very nice. It's a bit pricey but the food is very decent. You can have a lovely meal there and then make sure you stop off at the pub and listen to some music."

"Where is the pub?" I asked.

"At the hotel," she stated matter-of-factly, "there's only one pub in town."

I moved into the room and freshened up a bit. It was evening, and I was starving. Thank God the Irish eat later than most Americans.

I went back to the pub. I entered from the lobby through wood doors with glass inlaid on the upper half of each. The pub was a large room with wood paneling, a low ceiling, a fireplace against the far wall, and a bar that was L-shaped. It looked every bit the part of a small Irish mountain town pub.

There was a group of five young guys watching a football game on the television. They were cheering and having a good time, totally absorbed in the game. There was a woman sitting at the bar. She had obviously ordered dinner there and was finishing up. She had blond hair and appeared to be close to my age, maybe late forties or early fifties. Across the bar and kitty-corner from her was an older gentleman drinking a beer. Behind the bar was the bartender, another gentleman in his late fifties or early sixties, with white hair, white beard, a little scraggly-looking, and a bit craggy in the face.

I walked up to the bar next to the woman and ordered a pint of Guinness. I turned to her and said, "Do you mind if I take the stool next to you?"

She smiled. "No, not at all."

I sat down and introduced myself. "What a day," I said. "I had no intention of being here tonight. I spent the whole day being lost and I just happened to be in this town."

"I'm Sofia," she said. "I wasn't supposed to be here either. I'm supposed to be on a plane out of Dublin to L.A. to meet with my agent, but with the hurricane coming in, all the flights were grounded. Since I have an open ticket, I decided to stay a few more days and wait it out."

"That's pretty cool that you have an open-ended ticket," I said.

"Yes. I've been gone a long time. I've been on the road for five weeks so far."

"Wow! How so??"

"I'm a writer and I've been doing research on a book. I'm writing about the Irish. Actually, more about the Celts," she replied.

My interest was completely piqued.

"That's fascinating," I said. "I'm here on vacation and doing a little personal exploration writing. Please, tell me more about your book."

She looked down at her plate, uncomfortable. "I don't know if I want to, since you're a writer. I wouldn't want you stealing my ideas."

I laughed. "Oh my! No, seriously, I'm not a writer."

She looked at me and decided I was telling the truth. Her eyes lit up and she smiled.

"It's a mystery novel and it centers around finding an ancient Celtic artifact that has been lost to time. The story begins with a young professor searching for it from the time of the Celts in Greece, through Europe, up through Scotland, then down into Ireland."

"That's really cool. I can't wait to read it," I said.

She started to tell me about some other things she had done. As I listened to her, I felt the presence of someone next to me and I turned my head to the left. There was a young man in his early thirties who had come up and ordered a Guinness. But the bartender didn't pull him a pint. Instead he went over to the right of the bar, reached underneath, opened a cabinet door, and pulled out a bottle. I was fascinated that he would choose to drink it that way. I looked at him closely. He had sandy hair, a beard, and very kind blue eyes. In his hand, he held a book.

He smiled. Instead of leaving with his beer, he leaned over and said softly, "I couldn't help overhearing, are you writers?"

"I'm not the writer, she is the writer." I gestured over to Sofia.

"Fascinating, do you mind if I join you for a bit?" he asked.

We looked at each other and nodded in agreement.

"I'm Allen," he said.

I smiled. "I'm Nancy and this is Sofia."

As Sofia explained her book to him, I saw his eyes light up. I drew in my breath as I could have sworn they looked like fire for an instant.

"Of course," he said. "There is so much mythology about the Celts originating out of Greece before traveling across France and eventually to Scotland and Ireland."

"Yes!" Sofia exclaimed. "I've been up in Scotland on the outer Islands because, as you know, there are a bunch of the standing stones. I use them as guideposts of the Celts' journey and of this artifact down into the west side of Ireland where the story is going to end."

"I love the connection you are marking with the Celts' presence in Greece," he softly stated.

"Why?" I asked.

Allen took a drink from his beer. Slowly and methodically, he wiped the foam from his beard.

"It is believed that the Celts originated in central Europe. We know they interacted with the ancient Greeks. There were battles between them that were recorded by the Greeks. The Celts were nomadic and moved through Europe. Some ended up in Scotland, England, and Ireland. But I believe the Celts had a stronger connection with the Greeks other than through warfare. I think they share more with regard to language and culture."

"What are standing stones?" I asked.

"They were essentially markers of a chieftain's territory. The remaining ones that have been found intact suggest they were usually about a meter tall and rectangular. On the corners, marks were made that usually spelled out a ruler's or clan's name. Some laid out the lineage of certain chieftains," Allen explained.

He reached out and grabbed a pad of paper with the hotel's name on it off the bar.

"I'll show you," he said. "Do either of you have a pen?"

I reached into my satchel and pulled one out.

"Here," I said.

Allen took it and proceeded to draw a rectangular image on the bottom half of the paper. On the corners, he drew slash marks of different lengths and closeness. The marks went the length of the rectangle.

My eyes widened as I recognized the image. "I've seen this before!" I exclaimed. "It was in the National Antiquities Museum in Dublin. I think it was called Ogham?"

I pronounced it as Og-ham. Allen smiled, but his eyes told me I had said it wrong.

"It's actually pronounced more like *ow-uhm*. The *h* silences the consonant before it. And it's based on the name of the god of poetry, Ogma."

Allen drew multiple line characters on the top half of the page. Each line was different. Some had lines that crossed or had marks of different amounts and lengths on one side of them. On top of each of these lines, he then placed a letter of the alphabet.

"So, this is the Ogham alphabet," he said. "Each line represents a character of the alphabet. When one reads the stones, you start at the bottom and spell upward to the top. As you can see, it's a cumbersome writing style."

Both Sofia and I sat transfixed by this young man. Once again, I was being led back into Ireland's ancient past by his effortless ability to explain such esoteric knowledge. As for Sofia, this man was explaining and affirming the basis of her book.

Allen motioned the bartender for another beer. Once again, he was served a bottle of Guinness from the cabinet below the bar. Allen took a sip and continued.

"There are many theories about the origin and the use of Ogham as a written language. The earlier, popular theories espoused that its connection is to Latin, either as an attempt to make a written Irish language or to hide the Irish language from the priests. But I don't believe that's true. I think the origins came from Greece."

Both Sofia and I sat silent. He continued.

"However, I believe that once the Irish were exposed to Latin and its ease of use, they readily embraced it. Latin could express much more depth, more emotion than their old way of writing. It was easier. That's why I don't think Ogham was used to hide the Irish language. Rather, it predated the introduction of Latin. And as we all know, the Irish were and are to this day very much into expressing themselves through art."

I took a drink of my beer and thought about what I had just learned. The Irish were already a literate culture prior to the Christian monk's arrival. I thought back on the Book of Kells exhibit. That scriptoriums flourished here in Ireland now seemed self-evident. It was already a culture that valued the written word. Another example of the blending of the old and new ways.

As an American, my historical perception of a meeting of cultures involves conflict, bloodshed, and subjugation. I didn't realize until just now that there could be a history of such events that were not violent, and in fact harmonious. Maybe there was a stronger embrace of new ways and cultures back in the fourth and fifth centuries that didn't exist anymore and hasn't for a very long time.

As I had been silently contemplating all of this, Allen and Sofia had moved on in the conversation and were talking about the origin of words. Eventually, Allen turned toward the formation of surnames and the tracing of a lineage. I sat transfixed, listening to the connections and evolutions of words and meanings through languages and cultures that both he and Sofia were making. I leaned in, absorbed by this conversation. This is what I had come for, this was what I was looking for.

Allen saw my interest and asked. "So why are you here in Ireland?"

I looked around the bar, back to him, and said with deep sincerity, "I'm here to find myself, to find my past, to find my connection with something greater, and I guess I believe I will find it here."

I felt embarrassed as the words left my mouth. I looked at my beer, waiting for the gaffs and laughter. But they didn't come. Instead, I heard Allen's kind voice ask, "What is your family name?"

Oh, geez, what name should I say? I thought. I decided to start with my mother's family names. "My mother is a Redmond and a Kearns," I said.

"Oh, Redmond, that's a very popular name in this area," Allen said. "Have you met with any relations yet?"

"No, I haven't. The fact is I haven't done any research to find them. At least not yet." I felt even more stupid. Why hadn't I looked for distant relations? It seemed so evident now that I should have, but until this moment I hadn't even considered doing it.

"Well, I'm sure you'll find some. It's a very prominent name in these parts." Allen took a sip from his bottle and wiped his beard. He talked some more about historical Redmond figures. Then he softly said, "What is your father's name?"

Good God! He can read me like an open book. I squirmed in my seat. I have the worst Irish last name.

"Well, it's Britt. I know, not a very good Irish name," I said defeatedly.

I looked at Allen and again I saw kindness in his eyes. I looked at Sofia and saw her smile.

"That's a wonderful last name. Very Irish," Allen firmly stated.

"Yes, it is," Sofia affirmed. "It's a very old name."

"Really?" I said, surprised.

Allen tore another sheet of paper off the pad. At the top of it he wrote Breatainach. Underneath that, he wrote Briton.

"So, *Breatainach* is the old way of saying *Britannia*," Allen explained. He then drew a slash line between *Breatain* and *ach*. The slash line stopped on the word he had written below. "Over time the *ach* was dropped and then eventually the word was shortened to Briton."

Allen then drew two lines under *Brit* and a single line under *on*.

"Your name literally means 'Man of Briton,' and by that, I mean ancient Briton. The Briton that predates the Anglo-Saxons and the Romans. Your name refers to your family's descent from the original people of Breatainach. And Breatainach was the old Irish name for all the lands of England, Wales, Scotland, and Ireland. Yours is a very old name."

I sat dumbfounded at this new knowledge, absorbing what Allen had said. I had spent most of my life thinking I got the worst name in Irish history, named after an oppressor. That someone in Ireland would see my name as something to be proud of was mind-blowing.

I heard the boys erupt in cheers behind me. Sounded like their team scored a goal. I looked across the bar to the older man, sitting by himself with his pint of Guinness. He just sat there, staring ahead. The bartender was rubbing a glass dry with a towel, looking over at the game on the television. It was just a normal night at the pub, but my world was pitching about like a boat in rough seas.

As I refocused, I heard Allen and Sofia talking more about her book. Sofia motioned for the bartender and ordered a whiskey. I got another pint. I needed to talk to both of them more, especially Allen. I felt like I was in a movie. This whole day seemed so surreal.

Please God, let me remember at least a tenth of this night, I silently prayed.

Realizing that she too was going to be staying for a bit, Sofia excused herself and went to get her dog out of the car and bring it into the pub. I looked at this mysterious young man who seemed far wiser than his years warranted. This young man who had just gifted me a sense of self with his explanation of my last name. I wondered what he did for a living. I thought he had to be a professor or at least a graduate student, maybe in Irish history or literature.

"Do you work up at the park?" I asked.

"Oh no. I work in Dublin."

Aha! I bet he works at a college or university, I thought.

"Isn't that a bit of a commute?"

Allen smiled. "I actually work on the south end of Dublin. So it's not a bad drive. "

"At the risk of acting totally American, can I ask what you do?" I asked.

He laughed. "No, it's perfectly alright. I clean the beaches."

Bullshit! I thought. Still skeptical, I asked, "How do you know all of this?"

He grew very still and looked at his bottle of beer. His eyes were in a distant place, a distant time.

"My grandmother lived the old ways. I was very close to her and she would tell me stories. She knew many things. I would sit with her, and she would tell me about how it used to be before the English, before the Catholics, even before the Celts."

He took a pull from his beer. Slowly and methodically, he wiped his beard. I stayed silent. I knew he had more to tell.

"She meant so much to me. After she passed, I promised her I would not let the knowledge die with her," he said.

We looked into each other's eyes. I knew that level of grief; I knew that level of loss. At that moment we knew each other. He leaned in and started to say something when the pub door flew open and Sofia came flying in, dragged by her dog.

It was a very happy Australian sheepdog who, released from the isolation of the car, was hell-bent on meeting everyone in the pub. Allen and I burst into laughter. Sofia was alternating between trying to introduce her dog and swearing at him. The lads watching the game gave the dog an enthusiastic greeting. Even the old man across the bar smiled. Eventually, she got him to settle down by her stool and she resumed her seat between us.

As Sofia talked about her dog and their adventures, I started to feel tired. It had been a long day. I noticed that the game had ended and now only a couple of the young lads were still in the pub. The old man across from me was now joined by another older man and they were deep in conversation. One of the men was gesturing with his hands as he talked. I smiled and thought, *I bet that's a good story going on over there.*

I resolved to finish my beer and call it a night. I wanted to write down all these memorable conversations before I went to sleep. I knew I would lose too much of what had been discussed if I waited until the morning. The connection would be lost. The nuance would be lost. The magic would disappear. What I felt here in this pub was overwhelming. I was part of these people. I knew this place. I felt like I had never felt before in my life. It was otherworldly and I feared I would wake up with amnesia and never be able to tell of this night.

Sofia's dog started to fuss. He just wasn't comfortable. She got up and took him back out to sleep in her car. As she left the pub, Allen looked over to me and leaned in again. I knew instinctively he was going back to what he wanted to tell me before.

"You know," he said in a low tone. "There were others here before the Celts arrived. Back when men called themselves Breatainach."

I drew in a deep breath.

"Yes, there were others. There were humans and there were other beings. Today we call them fairies. But they were not harmless little glowing creatures. They were fierce. They were strong. And they fought. For hundreds of years, the conflict existed. Both sides suffered. Eventually, after four hundred years of fighting, a truce was established. It was agreed that the others would move into another realm, behind a veil."

I couldn't believe this. We were talking fairies, yet he was so serious, and I knew in my soul he was telling the truth. He looked intensely into me. Everything became still. It was important that I understood. And inexplicably, I did understand.

"But sometimes the veil thinned, and we interacted," I said soberly.

"Yes. Sometimes violently. But other times not," he whispered.

Why is he telling me this? I wondered. I sensed that it felt important to him to share this, but the rational side of me questioned if maybe he was having a bit of the craic with me. Playing a joke on the gullible American.

As if he'd read my mind, he soberly continued.

"It's important that you understand this as you continue on your travels. This island is a magical place if you allow it."

"That veil. It still thins, doesn't it?" I said, trembling.

Allen looked directly into me and said just one word.

"Yes."

DAY FOUR

ARKLOW

ap...tap...tap.

Tap...tap, tap, tap.

I turned over on the pillow to face the window and listen to the rain. The sky was gray. The ladies at St. Kevin's had been right; the storm arrived here this morning.

I snuggled deeper into the bed. Once I got home from the pub last night, I immediately wrote down the night's events. By the time I finished, it was quite late. My mind felt as foggy as the sky through the window. I had no idea what time it was, and I didn't care to find out. I just wanted to lie here in my semi-dream state and relive the night.

Did it really happen? Was it really as incredible as I thought?

Even though I knew it had happened, my self-doubts and caustic rationalizations started to overwhelm me. My inner Doubting Thomas kicked into full swing.

You had a few beers; you're probably overblowing the night.

Well, wasn't that convenient. Your first night out of Dublin and you had the experience you longed for. Seriously, Britt, that's so cliché.

You're pathetic.

I turned over and tried to stop the monologue in my head. I reached over to my journal on the nightstand. As I read my entry from the night before, the doubts faded away. Yes, it really did happen. Yes, it really was as incredible as I thought. And for reasons unexplained, yes, it really was connected to this journey.

I looked up at the ceiling and smiled. What the heck was I going to do today? I was completely off my schedule, and I could see that it was going to be a rainy day.

Well, I'll figure it out over breakfast, I told myself as I got out of bed.

After I got ready, I went into the breakfast room. There was one other couple in there and we smiled and said good morning. That was the extent of our conversation, being that they spoke very little English, and I spoke no German.

I took a seat and grabbed the menu card on the table. A man entered and walked over to me.

"I'm John," he said cheerfully. "So, you got the menu, I see. Look it over and mark what you want, and I'll be back shortly to pick it up. Would you like some coffee? Or tea?"

"Oh, coffee please!"

I looked over the menu and made my selection. I opened my travel book and looked at my sightseeing options for the day. I decided I wanted to go to Arklow to see the lighthouse there. It was this funky modern-looking object, and I thought it would be fun to see it up close. Also, I wanted to head toward the coast. Because I don't do anything sensibly, heading to the coast as a hurricane was coming in sounded like a perfect outing to me.

John came back and started to clear the table where the other couple had been eating.

"Excuse me, but can I ask you for an opinion?" I asked.

He turned and looked a bit surprised. "Sure."

"If you had to choose between Wexford or Waterford to stay the night, which would you choose?"

"Oh, definitely Wexford for me."

"Why?"

"Well, we like the medieval feel about Wexford." He gestured toward the kitchen where Deirdre was cooking. "I mean, Waterford is nice and has loads to do. But I just like that Wexford is a bit off the tourist track. And I love the old winding streets."

"Okay, thanks."

I finished breakfast, went to my room, and packed up my belongings. I said my goodbyes and thanked them both for their hospitality. They wished me safe travels and cautioned me to be careful with the storm coming in. Deirdre told me how to get back out on the road to take me south to Wexford. John helped me get my bags in the car. By the time I was back alone in the car, I felt like I was leaving a distant relative's home.

To me, the day was breathtakingly beautiful. The grey sky brought out the green of the grass. The trees stood vibrant against the grey backdrop with a mixture of green, yellow, and red leaves. The rain, when it came down, was soft. As the narrow road wove itself through the mountains and valleys, it also wove an enchantment around me. The Island had me bewitched and I followed her as she led me through her countryside. I belonged to her today.

I drove through Avondale Forest, through the Vale of Avoca, and eventually made my way to Arklow. It was still early, and morning traffic was heavy. As I drove into town, I noticed a huge cathedral up on a hill overlooking the town and the harbor.

"I gotta check that out," I said out loud.

Eventually, after a series of mistakes and near misses on the road, I made my way to the marina where the lighthouse stood was. It was a private marina and appeared to be closed to the public that day. The area was very quiet, and it looked like everyone had moored their boats in preparation for the incoming storm. There were many empty parking spots that had signs limiting them to only members of the marina. Recalling the saying "fortune favors the bold," I pulled into one and got out like I belonged there.

A man exited the building and walked toward me. *Shit!* I thought as I braced myself for the confrontation, but he just smiled and walked by and got into a car. I exhaled, turned, and started to walk along the boardwalk with a huge grin on my face.

I love boats and water. I have often thought that if I hadn't made the decision to work with horses, I would have lived and worked on the water. The sky was overcast, and the wind was starting to pick up. I followed the road that bordered the marina. I saw abandoned industrial buildings and grass growing up through cracks in the asphalt. Combined with the overcast sky, the area had a depressing feeling. Here was the backstory of Ireland's economic struggles.

I stared at the hollowed-out warehouse in front of me. She was a massive structure, standing at least eight stories high. Some of her windows were gone and a portion of her siding had been ripped off. Parts of her roof had also blown away and rust stains streaked down her white side like tears. Unkempt hedges grew large and wild against her, and off to her side stood a lone smokestack. Here was another ruin of Ireland's past. As I looked upon her, I imagined the struggles of those who had worked here.

This was not the tourist side of Ireland. This was Ireland before the big technology corporations came, before the tourism boom. This was the Ireland of the working class; the people who struggled to make the rent, to buy food, to send their children to school.

As I walked back to my car, I allowed myself to see how the marina had probably looked when that warehouse was up and running. Instead of weekend sailing boats, I saw trawlers. I heard the shouts of men as they unloaded their catch of the day. I heard the silence of those whose day had not gone so well, and, as they secured their boats for the night, prayed that tomorrow fortune would smile on them.

I looked at the funny-looking lighthouse, with its red metal pole and lightbulb-shaped top. It was not a romantic structure. No love stories were going to center around it. But as I looked upon its utilitarian form, I wondered how many fishermen had it safely guided home?

I got back to the car and decided to check out the huge cathedral on the hill overlooking the city. I got my phone out and attempted to find the address. Weirdly, although the church could be found, no address was listed in any of the sites I pulled up.

"Well, how hard can it be to find? It's huge," I said.

I drove back over the bridge and headed toward the church. Forty minutes later and too many U-turns to count, I was still unable to find an entrance. I drove all around the building, but there wasn't one road that led up to it, nor was there anywhere to park and walk in. Frustrated that I couldn't accomplish this seemingly simple task, I gave up and decided to continue on my way toward Wexford. As I drove down a road to connect with the route out of town, I came upon another impressive church. Quickly, I pulled into the small parking lot next to it.

"Fuck it, I'm going to go into a church!" I said.

As I stomped up toward the entrance, I stopped to look at what appeared to be a sarcophagus lid. The plaque next to it said that although the cross inscription was from the thirteenth century, the shape of the slab suggested it was considerably older. The cross was crude and looked like it was an attempt to incorporate a more ancient symbol into its design. It also stated that it was located on the north side of the Arklow Bridge, which was where the marina was located; the area I had just walked around. As I read this, I exhaled and let go of my anger. I closed my eyes and settled my thoughts.

I have to stop. I have to stop being so driven, so goal-oriented. Something greater is communicating with me.

I looked at the steps leading up into the church, a Catholic church, and I knew this was the one I was meant to visit. I entered a foyer and then through the doors. I was immediately struck by how bright and cheerful the church was. The ceiling was in the shape of a dome which created a spacious feel. The walls were painted a soft yellow. The place exuded warmth and openness.

A couple of older ladies were busy cleaning the pews and I heard someone with a vacuum cleaner off to my left. I genuflected and did the sign of the cross. Cautiously, I walked up the center aisle, taking in the feel of the place. One of the ladies cleaning the pews was close to me.

"I hope I'm not intruding," I said.

She looked up and smiled. "Oh no. You are very welcome here."

"Your church has taken me by surprise. I wasn't prepared for how open and cheery it feels."

She beamed with pride at my compliments. She moved closer to me. "Yes, we are very proud of it. This church was built by the local fishermen. They donated the money. They struggled and sacrificed so we could have this wonderful place to worship."

Seeing my interest, she continued, "In fact, four priests of this parish are buried here, right under the center aisle. They were very important in getting this church built." She gestured toward the back of the church. They made sure this was a place of worship for everyone, not just the wealthy."

I turned around to see where she was pointing. Above the doors was a plaque. I looked with surprise as I read that two of the priests were Redmonds.

"Oh, wow! My grandmother was a Redmond," I said.

I felt her hand on my shoulder as I stared at the plaque.

"Well then, I guess you are meant to be here," she said.

With that, she moved off and continued with her cleaning. I continued to read and reread the plaque. I dropped my eyes to the wall underneath it and, off to the side, was another smaller sign. It felt like ice water was flowing through me as I read its simple message: "Seek and ye shall find."

THE FOREST

I returned to my car with more questions than answers. It was not lost on me that something had brought me there. Some unseen power was running the show today and I was just along for the ride. Now I was filled with an urge to get out of the city and go somewhere I could be outside, alone in nature. There was a bird refuge on the coast near Wexford and I entered the coordinates in my GPS.

As I drove southward, the conditions outside steadily deteriorated. Yet I continued on. It made no sense, but I needed to go toward the coast. Squalls were now coming ashore and at times it was difficult to see the road, the downpour was so heavy.

Eventually, I saw a sign for the bird refuge, but my GPS didn't tell me to exit. For the next quarter mile, I debated with myself on what I should do. Should I take the exit and disregard the GPS, or should I trust that it might be taking me on a more direct route? As the exit drew near, I was still in conflict.

Again, I felt something powerful in me, and realized a decision had been made. As I neared the exit, I stayed in my lane and continued. My hands on the steering wheel were shaking.

"What the fuck is going on with me? Now I'm listening to voices in my head." To top it off, I was now talking to myself. "Well, that's it, I'm finally going crazy."

As I drove into another squall, I laughed. This was madness. Yet I had never felt more sane. I felt purpose, though I didn't know for what. The world seemed so simple then. I was a supplicant to fate.

I looked at the darkening sky and wondered what the conditions would be like at the refuge. About fifteen minutes later, my GPS indicated that I was to take the next exit. I did and turned left onto a two-lane road. I weaved around open fields enclosed by stone walls. Eventually, I came to a crossroads. Here my GPS instructed me to turn right, and I headed through a small village composed mostly of stone buildings. The area had a timeless quality about it.

I drove out of it quickly and was back into a rural setting. But now instead of open fields, it was thickly forested. Occasionally, the forest would give ground to a marshy bog. The area was hilly, and I got more and more nervous that I wasn't getting any input from my GPS. I slowed down and quickly looked down at my phone. My suspicions were confirmed. I had no cell service. Once again, the second day in a row, I was flying blind.

I continued on regardless, but I knew I wasn't going to the bird refuge. Once again, I was being led somewhere else. This time I didn't resist and kept my eyes open for a sign. I had no idea what I was looking for, but I was certain that I would know it when I saw it.

I drove down a hill and the sides of the road widened out. On the left side of the road was a dirt patch with a car parked. I zoomed past and over a small bridge, but I didn't get very far before I felt that pull again. I needed to go back to that spot. That was it.

I turned around and drove back. I pulled in close to the other car.

Should I get out?

Is this really the wisest thing to do?

Through the rain-splattered windshield, I looked down the path before me and felt the tentacles of anxiety grip me.

"I know you brought me here, but I'm not sure I want to do this," I said timidly.

I heard the engine of the other car as it started up, the sound of its wheels on the gravel, and then silence. Even though I was apprehensive, I succumbed to the pull inside me to get out and go alone into that forest.

Quickly, before my doubts and fears took control, I exited the car, pulled on my rain jacket, and set out down the path. Trees towered over me and canopied the path. The rain fell softly on me as I walked down an incline and disappeared from the road. A stream was on my right and the path followed it. Autumn leaves strewed the wet pathway. As I walked on, I looked at the thick vegetation all around me. The place felt secluded and all I could hear was the soft fall of rain on the trees above me, the gurgle and swoosh of the water in the stream, and my own breath.

However, my nerves had not quieted down, and I vigilantly looked up the hill then toward the stream. Nothing. But still, I could not relax. I felt vulnerable. I felt exposed. I felt foolhardy. Yet I continued.

"Okay, this is what you came for," I said to myself. "You wanted to get out of your comfort level. You wanted an adventure."

I looked down at the path in front of me and stopped. Right before me was a mid-sized feather. It was black with white in the middle. I bent down and picked it up. It was not wet. I looked up into the trees. I heard and saw nothing. I looked back at the feather and smiled. This was a sign, and I knew I needed to press forward. I believe feathers are a sign from the Divine; a signal that one is on the correct path. An affirmation of sorts.

I stepped forward, this time with resolve. I breathed in deeply. I closed my eyes and smelled the tannin of the rotting wood, the mustiness of the soil. I listened to the water as it coursed its way toward the sea. I opened my eyes and noticed how beautiful and perfect this forest was. I was in another church. This was sacred ground.

Now I looked around out of wonder rather than fear. Again, before me was another feather. Just the same as the previous one, not wet and in perfect shape. I picked it up. I walked on and the path became more unkept, wilder. I didn't care that I was alone. I knew I would be. The path became narrower. The hillside felt like it was closing down on top of me. Ferns grew along the hillside and reached out. Everything felt thick and closed in. I came up to a small waterfall. It cascaded down the hillside over exposed granite, pooled, then overflowed again over more granite down toward the path. I looked down and again there was another feather just like the other two. I shivered, bent over, picked it up, and I thought of Allen. I was in a world behind a world.

"The veil is thin here," I whispered.

I continued and soon came upon a large, uprooted tree, covered in green moss. It had fallen across the stream. All of its bark was lost; only its large stripped-down limbs remained. It looked ethereal. I felt the urge to walk across it. It was a pathway. As I approached, I hesitated. I feared falling off. I felt disgusted with myself. There was a time I wouldn't have hesitated. But now? I felt old and useless. I thought of my younger self, who would have joyously and effortlessly scampered across. What happened to her?

I returned to the path and wiped tears of self-pity off my face. "Move on and don't get bogged down with the *should've, could've, would've* shit," I told myself.

I walked on and followed the stream. *How much longer was I going to go on?* I thought.

Before I could answer, whatever had brought me here answered me. The path made an abrupt turn over a stone bridge across the stream. I looked over the bridge and there was no path, only forest. Ahead of me were steep, thickly forested hillsides which converged together, separated only by the stream.

This was the end. Now I had to make a choice.

I could stop here and accept the ending set before me. I could turn around and head back to the car, all the while telling myself I had a nice little adventure, a soulful walk in the woods. That would be very comfortable. Very safe. But deep down, I knew I wasn't going to do that.

Instead, I just stood there. It was beautiful just being there looking at that bridge. The bridge was minimal in its construction. There were no sides and leaves carpeted its path. It just laid over the stream stripped down to its bare essentials, just like that moss-covered tree. I could hear the birds singing. The rain was light. All was serene.

My other choice was to cross over that bridge, to amend for my cowardice earlier of not accepting the path over the tree. The more I looked at the bridge, the more I realized there never really was a choice. I was meant to cross over.

I stepped onto the bridge and slowly made my way over. What before looked like a smooth pathway soon revealed itself to be over-grown with roots that spread from a lone tree at the other end of the bridge. They twisted and knotted around each other as they traversed the stone structure. So entwined, there seemed to be no separation between the two: bridge and tree, stone and wood, man and nature.

I looked down at the water flowing beneath me. It was deep here. Droplets of rain danced upon its surface, then just as quickly disappeared. No longer separate, they became part of the greater body of water, their distinctiveness lost in the whole of the many.

Carefully I stepped across, making sure I placed my feet in the spaces between the roots. It felt sacrilegious to step on them. I was entering a sacred realm and felt like all of my actions were being observed and judged.

I walked onto the grassy path on the other side of the bridge and toward the trees. I stopped at the edge of the grove. All was silent here. No longer could I hear the water. No birds sang from the trees. Just silence.

Apprehensively, I looked around but there was nothing. I felt like I was being watched. My heart slammed inside my chest. My breath quickened and the hairs on the back of my neck felt electrified.

"I'm afraid," I said softly to the forest before me.

I closed my eyes and concentrated on my breathing. As I breathed in, I felt a presence and heard the voice.

Do you fear the silence? Or yourself?

"Both," I answered.

In the silence, you cannot hide. What you fear, you fear of yourself.

I drew my breath in quickly. I felt a cold clammy grip upon my heart as fear seized her opportunity. My knees weakened and I sank down upon them on the wet grass. And there I stayed, unable to move.

I know what it is you fear,
what leaves you sleepless in the night.
The coldness of your bed.
The emptiness of your table.

The solitude of your heart grows with each passing year.
The passage of time is cruelly before you now, your youth and beauty fading.

The reality of your loneliness is clearly at hand,
and this you fear is your future.

Somewhere I heard a wail, then I realized it was me. The grip upon me released and I sank into the grass, sobbing. The truth spoken could not be denied. I was afraid. I was afraid of my loneliness. Brynn's rejection of me, Beth's death, my failed attempts at relationships, all came crashing down on me.

It seemed I couldn't be with the ones I loved, and I couldn't be happy with the ones who loved me. I feared the inevitable loneliness that seemed to loom before me.

I stayed in the grass, sobbing. I was alone. No one saw me as I wept. The rain joined me, and the clouds dropped down and enshrouded me in their mists.

WEXFORD

When I got back to the car, my outer jacket was completely soaked through. My body shook from the cold and the shock of what I had just encountered. The rain was steadily coming down now with no reprieve in sight. The storm had arrived.

As I sat waiting for the car heater to kick in, I closed my eyes. The confrontation with my fear of loneliness had unnerved me. The solitude of my existence lay keenly before me, alone in a car in a foreign land. The only sound was my rapid breath.

I reflected on what had just happened. How when I finally found the strength to rise up, I did not feel any cathartic release. No life-changing insight. I felt hollowed out, comfortless. There was no resolution or absolution. I didn't know if this voice was my friend or my enemy. Every time it came, I felt like I was losing my mind, unable to control the intrusion, or the biting truth of the words it spoke. Fresh tears fell as I recalled my pleas back there in the forest.

"Why did you bring me here? I don't want to be alone. Please, please help me. What do you want me to do?" I said, crying.

Only silence answered. There would be no explanation. Gradually, I became aware of the birds singing, the gurgle of the water as it flowed, the soft patter of rain on the leaves. Having fulfilled its task, the force that brought me to this place left.

I was alone.

I opened my eyes and looked out of the front windshield. The car heater was finally working, and its warmth was a welcome friend. As I wiped away the fresh tears, my stomach started to growl. It was time to head into Wexford and look for something to eat. I looked at my phone and noticed that I had cell service again. The weather wasn't getting any better. Perhaps it would be wise to get off the road for the day. I found a pub that offered lodging, entered the address, and drove away.

I wasn't that far from Wexford, but the rain and wind made the drive challenging. When I drove into town, the traffic became heavy on the narrow streets. Wexford, a medieval city, turned out to be a nightmare to navigate. The flow of traffic was faster than the input from my GPS and I missed turn after turn. To add to the difficulty, various streets were blocked off for repair. Eventually, I ended up on the outskirts of town on the same road I had previously taken in.

The rain was coming down hard and the wind was wild when I finally pulled into a parking lot. But despite the shitty weather conditions, people were still busy going about. I grabbed some coins out of the cup holder and paid for an hour. The parking area was next to a stone wall with a wrought iron gate. I looked through the gate and saw a graveyard and the remains of a building enclosed within it. There was a plaque on the outside that identified it as the remains of St. Patrick's Church. It seemed so out of place among the hustle and bustle of a vibrant city center. A relic, left out of time, out of place. The gate was locked, and it didn't look open to the public. It was just here, a sentinel of the past.

I started down the alley to Main Street. At the end, I finally saw the pub. I dashed across the street and hurried to the entrance. I ducked under the awning, closed my umbrella, and entered.

It was a place that had seen many days, most of them better. Dark wood and worn red velvet-covered wooden bench seats encased the place. I walked through the front area where a few elderly men were sitting. TVs blared; one had on a talk show and the other horse racing. Ahead through an archway was the bar. I walked over.

"Hello," I said to the bartender. "I'm looking for something to eat and possibly a room for the night."

"I can't get you anything to eat, we stopped that for the off-season," he said briskly.

"Oh, okay," I said, surprised.

"There's a pub down the street. They serve food."

"Uhm, okay, thanks."

I looked out the front window of the pub and watched the rain pouring down. What was I going to do? Nothing about this day was going right. Should I go down to that pub, get something to eat, then head onto Waterford?

I continued to stare out at the rain. The bartender moved on to other customers and was busy pulling pints. The wind was blowing, and the rain was hitting hard. I looked on and knew I had no desire to keep on driving today.

"Hey!" I shouted out to the bartender. "Do you still let rooms?"

"Yeah, we got rooms."

He dropped off the pints and came back to me.

"It's fifty euros for the night," he said.

"Okay. I'm parked at the car park up by St. Patrick's. Can I keep my car there or should I park someplace else?"

"Drive it on down and park in the loading area here in front. You can unload your bags. Then just go up that road." He pointed out the front window at the road that came down a hill to the intersection next to the pub. "At the top of the hill is a church, you can park there. You will be okay overnight."

I reached into my satchel and pulled out my wallet. As I was busy getting my money out, the bartender turned around and reached up and pulled a book down. He placed it on the bar in front of me. It looked old and had a hard cover. He opened it up where a ribbon marker had been inserted and I saw that it was an old-fashioned ledger.

"Name?" he asked without looking up.

"Nancy Britt," I stated.

He wrote it down in the ledger, made some other notations, and closed the book. He grabbed my fifty-euro bill off the counter and turned back around. In a seamless and efficient manner, he replaced the book on the shelf, opened the cash register, and deposited the money. Then he reached back in a nook behind the cash register and returned.

"You are in room 7. Here are your keys. So, what you want to do is go back out and to the right of the patio area is another door. This small key unlocks that door which gets you into the foyer where the rooms are located. This other key is your room key. When you leave in the morning, leave the keys in your room. The main door self-locks so make sure you have your keys on you when you go out."

I looked at the keys. One was a regular house key, which must be for the front door. It was the other key that really grabbed my attention. It was a skeleton key. Really? I put on what I hoped was a really good poker face as I took the keys.

In my haste to be off the road for the day, I hadn't really paid attention to the place. Now as I looked around, I noticed its rough character. The three old men in front of the TV weren't watching the horse races; they were filling out racing forms and running across the street to place bets. A rather large and intimidating man stood at the entrance to that establishment. The guy sitting in front of the other TV was passed out. The few other customers in the place were lost in their pints, staring at nothing as they drank.

As I headed back out the front door, my mind started racing. *Maybe this wasn't such a good idea. Oh my God, what was I thinking?* I exited the pub and saw the door to the right. I took a deep breath, squared my shoulders, walked past it, and continued on toward my car.

"Well, it's done now so I guess I just have to hope for the best," I said to myself.

I pulled into the loading area by the door to the rooms. I opened the front door and pulled my bag into the foyer of what was once a grand nineteenth-century building. There were a couple of doors to my right and ahead of me was an old staircase that wound itself upward in a graceful sweep.

I lifted up my bag and climbed the stairs. I made it up one flight of stairs and looked at the room numbers. It appeared I had another flight to go. Breathing heavier than I cared to admit, I picked up my bag again and proceeded up the next flight of stairs.

I reached the door to my room, placed the skeleton key into the lock and turned it. I heard the lock slide and pushed the door open. I looked in the narrow room. Two twin beds were crammed against one wall with about three feet between them and the side wall. Part of the passage space was overtaken by a small dresser which further crowded the room. A small box TV was up in the far corner and a small nightstand separated the two beds.

I grabbed my bag and lifted it in front of me, given that the passageway was too narrow to have it by my side, and entered the room. Off to my right was the bathroom, which was also small and very utilitarian in furnishing. A pedestal sink, a commode, a shower stall, and a single towel rack comprised the sole accouterments.

"Well, this room doesn't exceed my expectations, "I laughed, comparing it to my lodging the night before.

I grabbed the skeleton key off the bed and exited the room. I needed to get my car out of the loading zone before I got a ticket or towed. I trotted down the stairs, got in the car, and drove up the hill to the church to park.

The church was an impressive example of Gothic architecture, dominated by a huge spire in the front. Once again, I felt the sense of some force drawing me to it. A part of me didn't want to go in.

What painful truths did it wish to expose in here?

Somehow, I knew after my experience in the forest there was not an option in whether I would comply. Hesitantly, I walked over and stepped into the vestibule. It was a small space with stairs on either side that ascended to the balcony. In front of me was the door into the nave. I entered and stood transfixed.

It was built with the sole purpose to inspire, letting you know you had left the realm of the mundane. Now you were in the house of God. Or at least what humans believed it should be. The nave was arched all the way up to the dark wood ceiling. It had to be at least fifty feet above me, possibly more. At the far end of the nave stood the altar. Behind the altar and above it was an elaborate stained-glass edifice. It too was arch-shaped and encompassed most of the back wall. White marble pillars marched down the aisle and in between them were rows of wooden pews.

It was dark with only a few lights on. Despite the overcast conditions, there was enough ambient light from outside to illuminate the stained-glass windows, giving the place an ethereal glow. Once again, I was on holy ground.

Only one other soul was there with me. A lone figure sat in the middle of the nave, head bent down, wearing a white coat with a hood. It was deathly silent. Hastily, I dipped my fingers into the holy water and blessed myself. I walked up a few pews and then sat down. The creaking of the pew as I sat echoed forth and I cringed. But the lone figure remained the same. No shift in position, no lifting of the head, no acknowledgment of my presence.

After the day's events, especially what had happened in the forest, I felt the need to sit in contemplation. I stared at the magnificent stained-glass window behind the altar. I listened to my breath as I looked on. I felt anxious. I didn't know if I wanted another encounter with whatever it was that seem bent on interjecting itself upon me.

Just breathe, nothing more, just breathe.

Eventually, my mind settled, my shoulders dropped, and my body relaxed. I continued to stare at the window. Slowly it seemed to grow brighter, the blues, reds, gold, and greens vibrating with intensity. Shafts of brilliant white light began to emit forth, reaching out into the space and carrying the other colors along. Before my mind's eye was a kaleidoscope, a divine spectrum.

As the lights shimmered and danced, I felt nothing but joy. The darkness around me receded as the shafts of light shot forth. It was beautiful, and as I sat staring into it, a feeling of peace filled me. I didn't want to think. I didn't want to move. I just wanted this moment to last forever.

Then, just as quickly as it had started, the lights pulled back once again to the stained glass behind the altar and in their wake, the darkness returned. I blinked and refocused on my immediate surroundings. The cowled figure before me remained unmoved, head still bent in prayer, seemingly oblivious to what I could only feebly describe as a miraculous light show.

Perhaps this was a common phenomenon here, nothing more than the simple refractory effect of sunlight on the window. Maybe I just made it more than it was, wanting comfort and solace after my experience in the forest.

Or maybe, just maybe, my hooded companion here summoned this apparition, and being a true believer, had no need for justifications or rationalizations as I did.

All I could say with certainty was that as I now sat in the darkened nave in the muted glow of the stained-glass windows, I felt small. The warmth of the light was gone, and the damp chill of the day was once again upon me. Realizing the pattern of the day, I knew that the force that brought me here had taken its leave, its purpose fulfilled.

I got up and briefly considered walking up past that mysterious figure but decided against it. Some things were better left unanswered.

The rain was coming down as I left the church, but I didn't go back to the car to get the umbrella. It felt good and I welcomed it hitting my face and dampening my hair. It connected me back to the present. I briskly walked down the hill to the pub, deeply breathing in the coldness of the air.

Not wanting to be alone, I went back to the pub and ordered a pint. I didn't want to hear that voice, and I especially didn't want to process the weird events of the day. I needed the company of strangers and the soothing numbness of alcohol. I sat at the bar silently, sipping my beer, and stared mindlessly at the rain.

THE STORM

After an incredible dinner at Cistín Eile, I decided to sit in the pub and write in my journal rather than go up to my room. It wasn't that late, and I still didn't feel like being alone. Despite the poor weather conditions, there were still a few customers. A football game was on two of the TVs, and the other TV was showing the news, which mostly covered the storm.

In the back area was a small group of twenty-year-olds, four guys and one woman. In fact, she and I were the only females in the establishment. In the front area, five older men were also watching the game, and another older man was sitting by himself, watching the news.

I ordered a whiskey and tucked into a corner booth. Situated so that I could see both groups, I could also look out the front window and watch the storm. I pulled my journal out of the satchel, took a sip of whiskey, and settled down to write.

What a difference twenty-four hours could make. Last night I was talking with Allen and Sofia about Celts, the roots of languages, and the subtleties of names across cultures. I learned the meaning of my surname and found a personal and ancient connection to Ireland. But most intriguing was Allen and his innate knowledge of the mysticism of this Island. I thought back on his confidences about fairies and the veils that separated the realms of men and spirits. Part of me wanted to laugh and think he was just having a bit of the craic with me. But then I remembered the look in his eyes, the seriousness in the tone of his voice, and I knew he wasn't joking. I took another sip and thought once again, *Was he real?*

Now I was holed up in a dive bar, riding out a hurricane with strangers. One of the young men in the back was shouting and cursing at the game. The young woman seemed unfazed by him as she sipped her pint and half-heartedly watched the TV. However, his violent outbursts unnerved me.

I tried to focus back on my journal, but my mind was as unsettled as the weather. I had my own storm brewing inside. My discomfort of being only one of two women here kept coming up. Rain slashed against the window, and the wind rattled the front door. It was very apparent that I was on my own if any situation arose. I knew well the darkness of men.

My mind wandered back to my first experience with that darkness. I was six years old, and my family had just moved to Salt Lake City. This was in the early 1970s. Back then it was still predominantly Mormon. My parents, being devout Catholics, sent me to parochial school. I had to walk three blocks to and from the bus stop. Dressed in my plaid uniform, I stuck out like a sore thumb. It didn't take long for a gang of boys to find me out. They were around ten or twelve years old. At first, it was just name-calling, but with each day they grew bolder. It didn't take long before they pushed me around, knocked me down, spat on me, took my school bag, and destroyed my homework.

This continued on a regular basis, and despite my tears and pleas to my parents, they did nothing. They could not believe that such acts of violence existed in this affluent part of town or that their neighbors' sons could be capable of such acts. It was easier for them to accept that I was exaggerating, that I was the one having a hard time fitting in. In their minds, it would all work itself out.

So, at the age of six, I realized that no one was going to help me. I would have to do it alone. The next time the gang came at me, I dropped my school bag and landed a hard punch on one of the boys. It was a good punch, and he staggered back. This momentarily stunned them, but only momentarily. Then as if some primal trigger had been pulled, they set upon me with a frightening ferocity. I fought as hard as I could, but given the age difference and the fact that there were four against one, I didn't stand a chance.

Blow after blow they struck. Eventually, two of them grabbed my arms, and the boy who I punched took out his anger as he repeatedly struck me in the face and the stomach.

"YOU FUCKING CATHOLIC CUNT!" he screamed at me. "You are going to pay for this!" His spit hit me in the face.

Suddenly I felt my skirt being lifted up and his hands grabbing at my panties. I was too young to know what was going on, but every instinct in me screamed out. I had to get away. I had to fight. Now it was primal for me. Every fiber in me recoiled. I knew this was terribly wrong, a wrong of a thousand generations. I felt his hand against my flesh, fumbling with more rage than purpose. The other boys shouted encouragement to him. I felt tears run down my face as I realized I was helpless to stop him.

I don't know how, but I managed to get in a kick, and it must have hit him in the balls. He dropped in pain, and I felt the grip on my arms go slack. I ripped free and ran as fast as I could. I didn't look back to see if they were chasing me. I couldn't afford to. I turned the last corner and saw my home about two houses away. Then disaster struck again as I hit gravel and went sliding on the pavement.

I rolled off the pavement onto the next-door neighbor's yard and lay there. I couldn't get up, and I remember just lying there waiting for them to catch up. But they never came. Tears streamed down my face. Weirdly, I felt pain and numbness simultaneously. Every time I tried to move my legs, the pain intensified. I looked and both my kneecaps were raw bloody messes.

I don't remember how it was all resolved. I know somehow my school bag got returned to me. I remember that for the rest of the school year, my mom either took me to school or met me at the bus stop after school. It was never talked about, as if by not acknowledging it, it would be as if it never happened. I would forget about it. But one does not forget such things and the scar on my right knee served as a constant reminder.

One thing that I had never been able to reconcile was that no one intervened. This happened in broad daylight, on a public sidewalk, in front of someone's house. Not one Mormon stay-at-home mom stepped out to help me, not one.

I took another sip of whiskey. It wasn't the last time I would be assaulted. Little did I know what other evil awaited me at the hands of men. I was raped at sixteen years of age by a man who I looked on as a father figure. As a young woman trying to break into the hunter-jumper business, more than once I was told that in order to ride the competitive horses, certain favors would be expected.

I looked out at the people all around me. No one cared about me. No one wanted to harm me. Not even the loud, brash young drunk in the back. I was just allowed to be. To be here with them. In this pub on a rainy night. No questions. No malice.

I looked into my whiskey glass and reflected on why I was here. I wanted to find an explanation, to tame my demons. For too long, I had accepted the lie that all the bad things that happened to me resulted from my own failings, some inherent fault within me. As I stared into the whiskey, I could hear the demons' whisper:

You allowed yourself to be in the wrong place at the wrong time.

Nice girls know their place.

How could you not be smart enough to see a grown man's ulterior motive?

Why should God give a shit about you when you don't?

You are weak.

It's because you're gay.

Now, as I sat alone in a bar thousands of miles from home, riding out a hurricane, it finally became clear. I swirled the whiskey in my glass, lost in the realization that not all demons are self-inflicted. Some are inflicted upon you.

DAY FIVE

THE TEMPEST

When I woke up, the sky was grey and rainy. The storm had made landfall during the night. Despite the dodgy accommodations, I slept very well. As I sipped my first cup of coffee, I looked through my travel books for things to do on the way to Waterford. I decided to go to the Hook peninsula and lighthouse. There were two reasons I wanted to do this. First, I really wanted to get to the coast and see the ocean. And second, once again the unnamed urge was in me, and it wanted me to go to the lighthouse. After that, I planned to go on to Waterford and end the day in or near Cork.

I left the skeleton key on the bed, grabbed my bags, and went down the stairs. I stepped out of the pub onto a quiet, rainy street. A few vendors were parked unloading goods for their stores. Otherwise, the place was deserted. I set off across the street and up the hill to the church parking lot. Dragging my bag up the two blocks was significantly harder than I thought it would be, but I made it and settled into the car. Churchgoers were arriving. I watched the people dash out of the rain into the church. Briefly, I considered joining them, but instead I started the car and pulled out of the parking lot. The rain, which had been a light drizzle, was now coming down harder as I made my way out of Wexford.

I traveled west and south toward the peninsula, and the rain grew in intensity. As I neared the coastline, the winds pushed the car around on the narrow road, and rain poured on the windshield with enough force that made it appear like a glass of water. The trees started to thin out, and large hedges were the only windbreaks. The landscape felt desolate.

As I passed Loftus Hall, I could see why the lone grey mansion was considered one of the most haunted places in Ireland. It certainly had a convincing backdrop. I thought of the various stories of how once, during a storm, the Devil appeared in the form of a handsome young man. He was invited to stay at the mansion and the Lord's daughter, Anne, became close to him. One night while playing cards, Anne bent down to pick up a card she had dropped. As she looked under the table, she saw that the man had a cloven foot. Upon Anne learning his true identity, the man became a fireball and went straight up through the roof, leaving a large hole in the ceiling. The legend further claimed that from this moment on, Anne was possessed and wasted away in her room waiting for his return. One thing that all the stories agree on was that Anne suffered from severe mental illness from that night until her death. We all have our devils.

The haunting of those who left too soon or did not love us as we needed.

The mansion had changed ownership over the years, and at one point it was even a convent. Each new tenant had stories of hauntings and supernatural phenomena. Today it was a tourist attraction. I pulled to the side of the road. As I looked out through the rain at the building set back off the road, the overcast sky blended into the cold grey stones of the manor and cast a gloom upon it. I saw it as my haunted house, the embodiment of my past; of choices made, consequences, and denials.

Oh, if only it could be that easy. If only we could set aside all our demons in a nice, enclosed structure, safe and well confined until, if we so chose, we could visit. But memories are as ethereal as ghosts and no barrier can stop them from slipping in and out of our minds. In reality, my ghosts roam the corridors and rooms at liberty, completely free to come back to taunt me when so inclined.

I started my way back to the lighthouse. But my thoughts kept drifting back to the ideas of spirits, reincarnation, life after death, and this mortal plane. This Island has always embraced the mystical, the spiritual, regardless of its form; pagan or Christian, old ways or New Age. I thought of Allen and our conversation the other night in Laragh. He spoke with such conviction, so much knowledge of the spirit realm. Once again, I wondered if he was of flesh and blood.

What do I believe? Have I ever truly believed in anything? Can I honestly call myself a spiritual person, a person of faith? I came here because I'm lost. A prodigal daughter returning home, looking for solace.

With these questions on my mind as I drove, I saw a sign that read *Templetown*. I slowed down and saw one building, Temple Inn. There was a large parking area adjacent to the building. Across the road and a bit south of the Inn were the ruins of a church. I made a mental note to stop on the way back and continued on toward the lighthouse.

As I approached the lighthouse, I was confronted with the majestic beauty of Ireland in her wild state. The force of the storm was unleashed on this bare stretch of land jutting out into the ocean. Fearsome waves crashed on the side of the cliffs and sprayed the road with seafoam. This was not a censored assault and not for the faint of heart. No barrier separated the road from the sea except the sheer drop of the cliffs. My heart pounded and I felt my senses come alive. No way was I going to turn back. Ahead, the lighthouse stood, the waves pounding up against the seawall. Water spewed up into the air as the wind drove upon the point with a savage fury. I felt like a traveler from a long-lost time who had reached the edge of the world. I pictured an ancient map inscribed with the dire warning: None but demons dwell beyond this point.

A handful of cars were in the parking lot when I pulled in. Because of the force of the wind, an umbrella would be useless, so I put on my layers and exited the car. By the time I made it to the lobby of the visitor center, I was soaked. I approached the fellow behind the register.

"When is the next tour?" I asked.

"Just missed one. The next one will be in a half an hour."

"How long does the tour take?"

"About thirty, forty minutes. That's because the steps up the lighthouse are narrow, we have to time it so groups don't run into one another."

I looked at the clock on the wall. It was already 10:30 and I still had Waterford and Cork to get to today. Sadly, I realized I wouldn't be able to stay. I smiled. "Thanks. Unfortunately, I can't do it. Would it be okay if I looked around?"

"Yeah, sure. We got a bit of stuff in here that gives some history. You just can't go into the lighthouse."

I thanked him again and turned around to go check out the room. On the way, I passed by a café where a handful of people were waiting for the next tour. The far wall was made up of windows that gave a view of the ocean and the cliffs of the peninsula, and what a view it was today. The ocean was a cold grey-green as it rose up in white-capped waves and crashed against the black cliffs. Seafoam flew up and onto the grass, so much that it looked like patches of snow.

This lighthouse was one of the oldest operating lighthouses in the world. In the back room were items used centuries ago for sea rescues. Looking at the ancient ropes and lifebuoys and seeing the condition of the sea outside, I couldn't fathom the bravery of the men who for over eight hundred years here had risked life and limb to go out in such horrible conditions to aid a fellow seaman.

I left the visitor center and headed toward the lighthouse and the sea just beyond it. I stopped just outside the doors leading into the tower, realizing I couldn't go in. I looked to my right and followed the path around the side of the building to the wall. On the other side of the wall was a small strip of land and rock, then the ocean. Waves were crashing up and over the wall, leaving pools of water.

Once again, I felt a familiarity, as if this was not the first time I had looked out from this point to the ocean. No other soul was outside with me. I watched the pull and push of the ocean as it broke upon the rocks. I didn't know why I was here; I just knew it was as it was supposed to be. I was in the moment, suspended from time. Nothing mattered but the smell of the water, the howl of the wind, and the rain on my face.

After what seemed like a long time, I became aware of others walking in my direction. This was my cue to leave. I got back in my car, but I knew I wasn't finished here. I drove back on the road, but after a few yards, I pulled over.

I walked out on the grassy ledge, at least a hundred feet above the raging sea. There I stood as the storm surged against the Irish Cliff. The ocean, driven mad, crashed on the stone cliffs. The wind whipped up the sea water and hurled it at me. The sting of it felt like a slap on my cheeks and tasted like tears as it streamed down my face.

I reflected back on Loftus Hall. I too had lived a haunted tale with someone who was not as she appeared on the surface. Rachael. The person I ended up in a relationship with after Beth. Ever since we parted, I tried to block her out. To forget, to deny. But here she was. In all her fury. Like a Banshee on the wind, she had found me, and was here to exact her revenge.

The mere thought of her drove me mad with anger, resentment, and fear. We lived together for twelve years. Twelve years that I would never get back. And here on this rocky outcrop, six years after I summoned the courage to stand up to her and leave, I was forced to reckon with her one last time.

> *To go forward you must go back*
> *Back to the time when your light almost went out*
> *Back to the time you grasped in the Darkness*

And cried out for no one
Believing none would hear

But here you are and a choice must be made
Will you cower in Darkness?
Or will you stand?

I faced toward the onslaught. No mercy was shown. I was knocked to the ground. The gates of Hell had been opened and the wind howled with the voices of the damned. On my knees, I looked at the grass, my limbs trembling. And then I felt it.

A strength I hadn't felt in years burned through me, driving me to my feet to face the storm. Just as I rose each time, Rachael beat me down. Now it was time to face the truth. The harsh truth, the truth I didn't want to admit to anyone, especially to myself.

She abused me.

And I allowed it.

I got together with Racheal for all the wrong reasons. It was three years after Beth's death and I just wanted to settle down. I was still lost, but too young to be alone. All my friends were coupled up and I thought I should do the same. I had forsaken love, but I thought it could be possible to be happy, content, just without passion. I was incapable of passion. I was too immature to realize my folly.

So, I settled on Rachael. And in the early years of our relationship, when she would rage at me, I accepted it because I felt guilty. I felt guilty that I was not in love with her. At first it worked. I would concede to her demands. I would accept her lies that everything that was wrong between us was my fault. But as the years wore on, her outbursts—which most times were just verbal, but occasionally physically violent—only succeeded in hardening my heart to her even more.

That's when I returned to my first love: horses. As I reconnected with them, my heart opened up. I started to make separate friends and one of those friends opened my heart again.

I remembered someone saying that to admit to something was to have ownership over it, and to have ownership was to have control. And control was the last thing Rachael ever wanted me to have.

In response to my realization, as if Rachael herself was in control, the storm lashed out at me, and I was struck with such a force that I fell backward onto the wet grass and slid toward the edge of the cliff.

Still down on the wet grass, I knew that all my storms within me had drawn me here, and here they were unleashed. My doubts, failures, faithlessness, cruelty, unkindness, destructiveness—all were set upon me. But also unleashed were my fears. My fears of pain, of loneliness, of longing. This was my tempest.

I rolled over and knelt on the ground. The howls of the wind deafened my protests, my excuses, my rationalizations. I could only hear the truth of my soul's voice. It spoke of my faithlessness, my conceit, my hubris. My cowardice. The sea sprayed on me the tears of those I had wronged. My family, my friends, my lovers, my enemies…and myself. My pain and heartbreak were no longer concealed. and my fears of love and trust ruthlessly laid bare. I was exposed for the coward I had been and my soul would have no more.

So, I bore the brunt of those gales and let them beat me down like the ruins of the Templar church I had passed on the way. I stayed there until all that was left was the crumbling walls, a hollowed-out shell. Stripped of my protections and defenses, I felt naked and exposed. It was only then that I was able to feel the spray of the sea and let it cleanse me.

And in this kneeling position, on these Irish cliffs, I surrendered.

I accepted with a humility I had never known before the grace that had brought me here. I accepted the love that I had denied, a love that has no boundaries, no judgments, no limitations. I accepted my failures and found my strength. I accepted my unkindness and cruelty and found compassion and empathy. I accepted forgiveness and found absolution.

Still on my knees, I felt my face wet. But this time it was from my own tears. Tears of redemption. Slowly I stood up, and having faced my tempest, I turned back from the edge. It was time now to move on.

TEMPLAR CHURCH

S oaking wet, numbly I drove back up the peninsula and returned to the old church ruins. I pulled across the road in the parking area of the Templar Inn. No cars were there, and the Inn appeared as abandoned as the old church. The rain had lightened up, but the sky was still a dark grey. A brass plaque on the stone wall stated that this was a church established by the Knights Templar and then taken over later by the Knights Hospitallers, their rivals, after Pope Clement V dissolved the Knights Templar through a series of papal bulls.

I looked around. No one was there, and I saw no signs saying to keep out. I flipped the latch on the iron gate and pushed it open. I stepped in and looked around. My heart was pounding in my chest as I closed the gate behind me and walked up the path to an opening in the ruin. Silence permeated the space. The only sound was my breath, which sounded extremely loud in the deathly stillness that surrounded me. I looked at the church. A tall stone tower was on my left—I guessed it was about three stories high—and on my right was the nave. The path led up to a vestibule between the two structures with a tall stone archway for its entrance.

I stepped up the two low stone steps through the stone archway. Suddenly above my head came a rush of movement. Simultaneously, I heard the piercing caws of two ravens swooping out of the entrance of the tower and flying directly at me. My heart leapt up in my throat as I stumbled to avoid being hit by them.

"Jesus Christ!" I exclaimed.

I felt the brush of their wings when they passed overhead, loudly complaining of or announcing my presence in their realm. I watched them pass through the nave and up over the walls. Quickly,

I turned back to my left, my fight-or-flight responses ready as I peered into the darkness of the opening to the tower.

No one and nothing appeared, and I let out my breath. My hands were shaking. I felt my body quiver as the adrenaline moved its way out. I caught my breath.

I stood there alone in the ruin. The stone walls of the entry, covered in moss and lichen, testified to the passage of time. Grass grew up along the stone floor and vines moved up the walls. In the remains of the nave, grass covered the ground in patches, intertwined with thickets of shrubs and vines. Broken window mullions remained in a few of the window openings. Plaster had fallen off the walls in various places, exposing the underlying stone.

I stared into the space, looking from wall to wall. I observed the ravages of time. I felt the presence of those who came here and knelt in supplication. I heard the prayers offered over the centuries. The cries for lost loves, broken promises, for forgiveness, for hope, for solace, for redemption. I looked around the space and what I saw was the earth claiming it back, yet the stones remained unmoved, man and nature locked in a timeless battle.

Or...perhaps not?

Yes, now I understood.

Here is where it was to happen. On the cliffs, I gave my confession, and here would be my absolution. In the ruins of a church. A church intertwined with nature. A church both dying and being reborn. A church very much alive.

I was no longer conflicted with doubt. For me, the divine resided in the plants, stones, and trees as much as it did in a cathedral, synagogue, or mosque. Then I heard her.

Was not the sparrow as much a messenger of God as the prophets who wandered the deserts?

I closed my eyes and breathed in. The voice no longer scared me. There were no absolutes that separated the physical and

149

spiritual, the carnal and holy, the present and past, the mystical or familiar.

I felt a glow of peace. Everything was still. No wind blew, no birds sang. All around me was silence. I was still too, comforted by the warmth of love that enveloped me. This time I felt the voice before I heard it.

I did not bring you here to learn about names, places, or dates. Nothing so trivial would interest me.

No, I did not summon you for such mundane tasks, for such small and insignificant matters.

You are my child. You were always destined to return. You are as much of this Island as the grass beneath your feet and the stones that surround you. You are of nature and you are of man.

But you have always belonged to me.

Time has no meaning; it is yesterday and it is tomorrow. You are a newborn suckling on my breast and the bones beneath the tomb.

The pain of our separation was born from desperation, from need, and from blood.

Over the centuries, over the distances of time and space, over the foreign lands you sought refuge in, I never forgot you.

Like lovers, we have yearned for each other. And when your soul cried out, I heard.

And so. I called you home.

KINDRED SPIRITS

I stopped talking and looked over at Jen. It was getting late.
"Gosh, look at the time. I've kept you later than you probably expected or wanted," I said.

Jen smiled and yawned. "Don't worry about it," she replied. "I'm enjoying your story and haven't noticed the time."

"You are kind, but I won't torture you anymore. I can finish this another day."

"What are you talking about?" Jen asked, surprised. "Is that all you are going to tell me? "

Sheepishly, I looked over at her and replied, "Oh no! There is definitely more. I guess I'm feeling a bit self-conscious keeping you here so late."

"Well, don't. Now I think we need a nightcap while you tell me the rest of your story."

With a grin on my face, I went inside and fetched two glasses and a bottle of Kilbeggan whiskey. I placed them on the table between us and poured a measure into the glasses.

"I believe Irish whiskey is the appropriate drink at this moment," I said, smiling as I handed her a glass.

Jen clinked her glass to mine. "To kindred spirits."

I chuckled and took a sip.

"What's so funny?"

"I was just thinking how funny you should use that phrase and how it relates to the rest of my day after leaving the Templar church.

"After everything I had gone through on the cliffs and in the Templar ruins, I was pretty much spent. I wanted to get to Cork, or more accurately Cobh, that night. But before that, there was one more place on my list for the day. I contemplated leaving it for the next day but once again I had that now familiar feeling telling me I needed to go to it today.

"Do you remember me telling you earlier about how the Choctaw Nation helped the Irish people during the Famine? Well, there was a sculpture in a town called Midleton that commemorated that act. It's called Kindred Spirits."

"Oh wow!" Jen replied.

I laughed. "Well, like most things on this trip, what should have been an easy and quick little side trip turned out to be something else.

<hr/>

I drove to Midleton with no problems. It was about five p.m. and evening traffic was heavy. But soon enough, I was driving past the sculpture.

It was in a park next to a river. But as I drove past, I couldn't see any entry point for the park. I continued on the road until I was past the park area. Then I found a place to turn around and head back, but I still couldn't find any place to pull over and park. Once again, I went past the sculpture. The road went under a bridge and on the other side was a parking area.

It was evening rush hour, and fighting with the traffic was time-consuming and frustrating. Eventually, I made it to the parking lot It was a nice area next to a river. A path led from the lot, and I started down it. I thought it shouldn't be far and I enjoyed the evening air as I walked.

I wasn't alone. There were joggers and others taking a walk. But after a short while I knew something was wrong. I should be seeing the sculpture by now. But all I saw were fields, wetlands, and the river.

I shook my head in disbelief. *How could I miss it?* I didn't know if I should continue on or turn back and see if I missed a side path that would take me where I wanted to go. I was lost and I just stood there, uncertain what I should do, all the while feeling frustrated and foolish.

Luckily there was, an older gentleman came walking up behind me. I swallowed my pride and asked him for directions.

"Excuse me sir, but I was wondering if you could help me?"

His face lit up and he had the best smile. It was infectious.

"You're from America,: he blurted out.

"Uhm…yes, yes I am."

"Oh, I love America! Such a wonderful country! My son lives there, he lives in Chicago. Are you from Chicago?"

"Uhm…no, no I'm not. I, uhm…I'm from Arizona."

"Oh ho! The Wild West. How wonderful! I just love America. Everyone is so nice. My son, he lives in Chicago. Been fifteen years now. Arizona, so interesting. Never been there, but I have been to Chicago. Wonderful, wonderful place."

Afraid I would burst out laughing, I looked away. He was so excited to meet an American. I couldn't get a word in edgewise as he told me all about his son. Listening to him go on about Chicago, I perceived the city from a completely different point of view. For me, it was just a large industrial Midwest city. But as I listened to this elderly man talk with fervor about all the wonderful things in Chicago, I realized that for him, Chicago was as exotic and cosmopolitan as Paris or Rome might be to an American.

Eventually, he slowed down and I seized the moment to break in.

"Actually, sir, I was wondering if you could help me find a way to the large sculpture? I can't seem to find my way to it."

"Of course, of course, you want to see it."

"Yes, I do. How do I get to it from here?"

"You can't."

"Sorry? I don't understand."

"You can't get to it from here, lass."

I stared at him, lost for words. *How can that be?*

154

"Did you park in the car park down there?" He gestured toward the way I had walked from.

"Yes."

"Well then, no problem. Just go back there and you have to walk down the road. That's the only way to get to it from here. The park will be just after you go under the bridge," he said encouragingly.

"Oh great! Thank you so much."

"No problem, lass. I hope you are having a wonderful vacation. God bless and God bless America."

With that, he left and continued on with his walk. I watched him move away from me. He had a slight stoop to his shoulders and the beginnings of an old man shuffle in his walk. But otherwise, he seemed quite spry. I smiled as I watched him move away. It felt good and comforting to talk to him. His enthusiasm for America was contagious, and for the first time on the trip, I felt a pang of homesickness and thought about my father.

He was a brilliant but intolerant man. Failure to live up to his expectations was met with cool indifference. I strove to be the best at whatever I did to keep in his favor. Unfortunately for me, what I was good at was not anything he valued. The sting of his disinterest in me beat me up harder than any slap or punch ever could.

It wasn't until I was in my forties that my father and I developed a close relationship. With age, he had mellowed out and changed, and honestly, so had I. Nonetheless, the scars were still there.

Now, he suffered from debilitating vertigo, which left him confined to either his bed or recliner for most of the day. Once a proud and vain man, he had always taken pride in his physical fitness. But as the days became weeks, and the weeks into months, I watched him decline, and sadness enveloped his soul. He now had fears and uncertainties, whereas there was only confidence before. Now, he relied on me heavily for all his needs. The tables had turned. And his frailty frightened me.

The old man had now walked out of sight, but I continued to look in his direction. I hoped he had someone at home to look after him. And for the first time on this trip, I worried about being so far away from my father. Not for myself but for him. And even though it had only been a matter of hours, my experience on the cliffs and in the Templar church had changed me. Now I felt an inner strength I hadn't felt before. The thought of caring for my father no longer frightened me. I knew now I could withstand whatever lay ahead on my journey with him through this final chapter of his. It was all going to be okay; no matter what happened, it was all going to be okay.

◙◙◙◙◙◙◙◙◙◙◙◙

I paused and sat silent, lost in that memory.

Jen broke the silence. "I remember when I had to care for my dad. It's a very intense time of life. And I found myself feeling guilty for taking time for myself. Which is so important to do when you are a caregiver."

I nodded in agreement. "I didn't feel guilty per se. I just felt an urgency to get back to him. I hadn't felt it before on this trip."

"So did you ever find your way?" Jen asked.

"I did as the man said, and soon I was at the sculpture. It consisted of nine stainless steel eagle feathers, each about twenty feet high, arranged in a circle. I subsequently learned that the arrangement was to represent a bowl of food."

"I never knew that the Choctaws helped the Irish and now I find out there is a statue dedicated to them in Ireland," Jen said in disbelief.

"I know what you mean. I went to parochial schools for eight years and was taught by Irish nuns. I heard all about how horrible the Famine was, but I never knew of the generosity of the Choctaws, who years previously had been forced to leave their lands in Alabama, Mississippi, and Louisiana and relocate to Oklahoma in what is now known as the Trail of Tears. They managed to send $170, which back then was a considerable amount of money. It's even more astonishing when you realize they did this after they had been subjected to their own diaspora. I found it very humbling as I realized their incredible compassion to help, despite the cruelty they had suffered caused, at least in part, by the hands of descendants of the very people they were helping.

"Other people and nations also sought to aid the Irish. A sultan of the Ottoman empire sent ships filled with food which the British government tried to blockade. Even Queen Victoria sent money for aid, an act in direct contrast to the draconian policies of her government.

"Yet these futile attempts at relief could not stem the tide of destruction and human suffering caused by the catastrophic potato crop failures and the callous indifference and ineptitude of government inaction. Ireland lost a quarter of its population in those four years, and the long-term effects caused mass emigration that led to further population declines for many decades afterward. Over six million men, women, and children emigrated between 1841 and 1900."

Soberly, I reflected that I am a descendant of that diaspora.

"As I walked around the sculpture, I noticed a white feather in front of me. I picked it up and saw it was a swan feather. I put it into the breast pocket of my coat. A little further ahead was another, and then another after that. I picked up each one and put them in my breast pocket as I made my way around the circumference of the sculpture. Four feathers in total.

"I remembered the spiritual symbolism of the four directions, the four seasons, the four elements, the four arms of the cross. I reflected on the earlier events of the day. The blending of the Christian and pagan in me. Now I stood gazing at a memorial that was significant to me both as Irish and American, the blending of both in me.

"Gratefully, I gazed up at the steel feathers. I felt peaceful. I felt whole. The swan feathers reminded me that I was loved and protected by higher forces. My ancestors were here with me. I was not on this journey alone. The force that kept directing and changing my path, the voice that spoke truth to me, spoke for a reason. The divine was here guiding me. It always had been, I just didn't realize it. More accurately, I didn't accept it until now."

"What a wonderful realization," Jens said. "It has been clear to me as you told the story that something else was at work. That you were being guided, so to say, on this journey. Such a powerful day."

"Yes, it was. Just one more peculiar thing to tell you about it.

"I decided not to go on to Cobh. It was getting late, and I was exhausted. I found a nice upscale hotel in Midleton to stay in. I decided to treat myself, especially after my accommodations the night before. After a nice dinner and a luxurious soak in the tub, I remembered the feathers were still in my coat's breast pocket. I decided to get them and let them air out before I put them in with my other feathers. I reached into the breast pocket, but nothing was there.

"I turned that coat inside out. But still no feathers. There were no holes either. There was no way they fell out. They were just gone.

"That night I had the most incredible dream. I was flying. I soared above a river, turned and skimmed the reeds along its banks, and as I glided, I could feel my muscles pull and lift me on the breeze. I looked out of the corner of my eye and saw that my arm was a wing of beautiful white feathers."

"After I woke up, I understood that this journey was about finding a way to love myself again.

"Now when I start to belittle or hate myself, I try and remind myself to close my eyes and feel the swan within me."

DAY SIX

GHOSTS

The next morning, I woke up to rain. My dream last night had left me feeling peaceful and happy. As I lay in bed, I felt different. A shift had happened. The angst, the longing for connection, and the sadness that had driven me to take this trip were no longer in the driver's seat.

I realized that I only had two more days in Ireland. At breakfast, I felt the now familiar urge, or force, come upon me. It wanted me to go to Kilkenny. So, it was settled. I also decided to stop and explore Jerpoint Abbey on my way there.

Jerpoint Abbey was built for the monks of the Cistercian Order in the twelfth century. It is considered one of the best examples of medieval architecture. The history nerd in me couldn't resist a visit. I looked out of the dining room windows. It was going to be another day outside in the rain among ruins.

Later, I was checked out of the hotel and in the car. I entered the address for the Abbey into the GPS and crossed my fingers that it would actually take me there. There was very light traffic coming out of town. I wasn't surprised. It was a rainy Saturday morning; most people were probably relaxing at home.

On my way out of town, I drove past residential neighborhoods. I could picture myself living here. An Irish suburbanite. I'd find a nice girl to settle down with. Enjoy a simple life. Go to the markets on the weekend. Meet up with friends for dinner. We would stay in bed on these rainy days, leisurely make love and snuggle in each other's arms.

Lost in this daydream, I drove into the countryside. The road was narrow, but not too bad. I drove past farms and through woodlands. Stone walls lined the sides of the road. A beautiful fall day.

The rain was sporadic along the way, sometimes heavy, other times soft. It seemed to take a long time, but eventually I arrived at Jerpoint Abbey. There was only one other car in the parking lot, which I soon discovered belonged to the woman running the visitor center. I went inside, paid the entrance fee, and went back out into the rain, overjoyed to have the place to myself.

I made my way over to the remains of the Abbey. Even in its advanced state of decay, it was impressive to look at. It must have been awe-inspiring in its youth. There were many tall stone Celtic crosses among the gravestones I walked through on my way up to the main building.

I crossed through the stone entryway and stepped onto a gravel walkway bordered by an ancient stone arcade that went around a large grassy cloister. On the columns of the arcade were carved stone figures. Some looked like knights, others were priests and bishops. One carving showed Madonna and child. But not all the figures were of this traditional type. Also among them were fantastical beasts, and in a moment of levity, I saw one that looked like a man with a stomachache.

Silently, I walked along the path. I looked through the columns across the grass toward the remains of the church and imagined what it must have been like to have been a monk here.

Well, it certainly would have been busier, I thought.

I walked to the end and turned right to start up the far side of the arcade toward the ruins of the church. A mist settled in, and it grew darker.

I stopped walking midway. I looked across the cloister but could barely see to the other side through the thickness of the mist. The hairs on my neck stood up. I wasn't alone anymore.

Quietly, you slip past the archways.

Solitary, a ghost among the ruins.

Humbly, you touch the stone. The cold on your hands opens up the tomb within. But only darkness greets you.

She does not lie here, for she is gone and cannot return.

Drink no more from this bitter glass, nor listen to the demons' subtle guile. Weep not these cruel tears.

Be not deceived, only death is a tenant of the crypt.

You love only a shadow.

My breathing became quick, and my heart drummed in my chest. There was no denying it. I knew.

I knew who the voice was speaking of. Beth. I remembered my promise to carry her memory within me. I was unwilling to let her die. At first, I wanted to be there in the shadows with her. In my dreams, she would come to me. We danced, laughed, and held each other, until eventually, she would fade away like the stars in the night sky. Each time I felt myself ache with a force that threatened to rip me apart.

As the years wore on, I dreamed less and less of her. But occasionally, I would meet her in my dreams. Other times I'd be doing something, and she would be there in my thoughts, or I'd be somewhere and think how much she'd enjoy what I was doing. I'd hear a song and she would be there. It's funny how someone becomes so ingrained in you, you cease to know it's happening. I had carried her with me all these years, not consciously, but I had.

She was my mistress, my lover, and my ghost.

I measured every subsequent lover against her memory and the shortcomings and failures that occurred in my relationships were judged by the standard of her perfection.

But who can compete with a ghost?

Her memory used to be a cloak I wrapped around me to keep me safe and warm. In there, I could nestle into the comfort of her. In there, I had known love. In there, I had been loved. But now the cloak had become threadbare, and it no longer kept me warm.

I looked into the void and spoke words I should have said years ago.

"I have to let you go," I said with tears streaming down my face. "I love you, but I have to let you go. I've been afraid. Afraid to love as I did with you. I didn't want to let you go, I still don't. But I want to live again. I want to love again. I want to be loved again."

And so, it was done. Here in the ruins of an abbey over four thousand miles away and two decades later, I laid Beth to rest.

KILKENNY

I drove into Kilkenny around 1:00 p.m. The town was bustling with activity of people walking everywhere, darting in and out of stores and pubs. Music could be heard everywhere as various buskers plied their trade. It was a picture-perfect setting of a Saturday afternoon.

I set out to explore the town. I knew I wanted to go to the castle, but as I walked over to it, I found myself intrigued by all the twisting side streets. Kilkenny was definitely a medieval city and loaded with tremendous charm.

The castle was an impressive structure located on a hilltop overlooking the city. The rain, which had let up for a bit, was back at it, so I hurried up the hill. Despite the weather conditions, it was very crowded, and I had to wait in line as we slowly queued in.

Once inside, I followed the line of tourists through the various rooms. The castle had been beautifully restored, but I couldn't get enthused. My heart just wasn't in it. Whereas before I would have taken time and been more in-depth in my examination, now I felt like I was on autopilot as I moved with the flow of humanity through each of the exhibits.

My time at Jerpoint had left me emotionally exhausted. I was tired from being out in the rain all morning, and I was hungry.

I got through the rest of the tour and made my way back down the hill toward the main area called the Medieval Mile. I decided to wander down the narrow streets and look for a place to eat. I came upon a pub called Kytelers Inn. The sign stated it was established in 1324.

I sat in a booth in a part of the establishment called the Tavern Bar, the original cellar and kitchen area of the inn. Although with its thick black rock walls and stone pillars, it felt more like a dungeon or a tomb.

I placed my order and thought I'd look for a place to stay while I ate. I got out my phone, but I couldn't get any cell service. The waitress returned with my drink.

"Excuse me," I said. "But I can't seem to get my phone to work, I was wondering…"

"Oh yeah, there's no service down here," she said, cutting me off. "Walls are too thick. You'll have to go out to the beer garden if you want to make a call."

Just as quickly as she set my beer down, she turned and set off to the next table.

Stupidly, I looked down at my now useless phone. My grand plan to find a place to sleep was now rendered impossible by twelfth-century architecture.

The place was loud with people laughing and talking. I took a sip of beer, now self-conscious of my solitude. As I sat silently, I started to feel the strain of the trip. I was tired. I was tired from being outside in the rain. I was tired of waltzing through the waves of my memories. I was tired of confronting myself. And, for the first time on this trip, I was lonely.

I just sat staring at the stone wall in front of me. Nobody knew me here. It didn't matter to them that I was alone, that I was feeling defeated. None of it mattered to anyone. And that invisibility was depressing.

My food came and I ate slowly. Once I finished, I felt better, and decided to get another drink and go out to the beer garden to drink it while I searched for a place for the night.

Later, I toured a bed and breakfast called Mena House. A woman named Katherine guided me. We walked down the hallway to the back of the house. Along the way, Katherine pointed out the breakfast room, explained how breakfast worked, and pointed out a table filled with brochures of various attractions. Her cheerful chatter brightened me up and my melancholy lifted.

The table with the brochures was next to a large picture window that looked out onto a beautiful rose garden. My room was just to the left on the other side of the stairway that led to the upper rooms. Given the age of the house and the location of the room, it appeared that it had been converted from a back storage area or mudroom.

I walked through the door and was pleased to discover my room also had a window that looked out into this lovely garden. However, she wasn't exaggerating when she said it was best suited to a single person. The room was very narrow with just enough room to walk past the end of the bed. But it had an ensuite and I could put my bag on one side of the floor next to the bed. I readily agreed to take it.

Katherine smiled. "Wonderful."

As I took the keys from her, I saw the now-familiar look of curiosity and I could tell she wanted to know why I was alone. I wasn't wrong.

"So, what brings you here? Work?"

"No, I'm on vacation. I'm almost done, one more day left."

"Oh my! I'd never have the courage. Good for you!"

I laughed. "Actually, I've really enjoyed doing this trip solo, in fact it kind of spoiled me for traveling with anyone else."

"Well, that's brilliant. I'd never be able to do it, but well done. I'd get too lonely. Did you? I mean don't you miss sharing it with someone special?"

I thought about my feelings at lunch. Yes, I had and yes, I did miss being able to share all the amazing things that happened on this trip. But I also knew I wouldn't have had those experiences if someone had been with me.

I looked at her with a mischievous twinkle in my eye. "You know, what I have come to realize is that I miss my dog."

Katherine looked momentarily stunned by my response and then burst out laughing.

"Oh, good Lord! Right you are!"

Later that evening, after a nap and a hot shower, I set off to have dinner and listen to some traditional (or trad as they say in Ireland) music. I sat at a long bench that ran the length of a back wall of a raised part of the dining hall. Along the bench were several small tables.

It was a good location. I was close enough to the music to enjoy it without it drowning out conversation. Not that I had anyone to talk to. On my right was another single woman who was busy on her phone. The table to my left was empty, but about ten minutes after I sat down, a woman and her son took it.

As I ate and listened to the music, I couldn't help but overhear the woman talking to her son. More like a monologue really. She kept trying to get him to engage with her and all she got was grunts in reply as he steadfastly stared at his phone.

"Come on, Michael, put down the phone. This place is so interesting. Come on, listen to the music. Oh, look at all the stuff on the walls. Look, look, there's a suit of armor. Oh gosh! Oh Michael, honey, put the phone down."

On and on she went, trying to get Michael's attention. I stole a sideways glance to see them. Michael was probably twelve or thirteen years old. The mother was a woman in her mid-to-late forties, trying to look like she was in her early thirties. She had bright blonde hair and I could tell she was attractive underneath the heavily-applied makeup. Her outfit looked like it was out of some fashion magazine spread on how to dress for a weekend in the countryside.

Outwardly she presented as a composed cosmopolitan woman. But her voice betrayed her. I know desperation when I hear it. She caught me looking at her and smiled. I smiled back and returned to my food and the music.

"Look how quaint this place is, Michael. Come on now, stop playing that game. Michael, Michael, stop it, stop it. This is getting embarrassing. Michael, sweetie…"

Before she could continue, Michael stood up abruptly.

"I'm going to the bathroom." With that he left, phone in hand.

I looked up as he left the table and shot a glance over to the woman. She was taking a healthy swallow from her white wine. She saw me and smiled again. But her eyes squinted too much, and her lips were drawn too tight. She was not okay.

"He's at a hard age," I said kindly.

She leaned back against the bench and let out a sigh. This time when she looked and smiled at me there was a sense of relief and gratitude in her eyes. She knew I wasn't judging her. "It's my weekend. I just wanted to do something special, have a weekend getaway. Just the two of us."

She took another sip of her wine. I stayed silent. She set her glass down and ran her fingers up and down the stem, caressing it.

"Stupid. Just stupid of me. I thought if we got away, just the two of us, it would be like it was before."

She broke off and took a deep breath.

"Like it was before you were divorced," I said. "Funny, we think we can just move on, that only one thing has changed. That everything else will be like it was before. But it's not, it can't be. Like ripples in the water, we bob about and get pushed around. When the water calms down, everything is on a different track."

"Are you divorced too?" she asked.

"Me? No, no...well, yes...but no, no, not like that. But I'm here because, like you, I'm trying to pick up the pieces."

She grabbed her wine glass and slid across the bench closer to me.

"I'm Sorcha. Where are you from?"

"I'm Nancy. The United States, specifically Arizona."

She picked up her glass and raised it to her mouth. She gave a sly smile and teasingly said, "Why are you here?"

It was my turn to look at my drink. How should I answer that? *Oh shit, just tell her the truth,* I thought.

"There have been two women I've been truly in love with, in my life, and both times I lost them. Each turned my life upside down, but for completely different reasons. I came here to reconnect. I thought it would help to reconnect with my heritage. But really, I came here to reconnect to me."

Momentarily she looked shocked but quickly composed herself.

"I'm sorry." Sorcha's eyes had a compassion in them of someone who understood loss.

"Thanks. One died quite young. We were in our twenties. Devastated me." I paused and swallowed hard. "Today I finally let her go."

Silence.

Sorcha looked out across the room. When she turned back to me, I could tell she was going to tell me something that she didn't often disclose. "James and I met in college. First man I slept with. God, I loved him, at least at first. We married and I worked while he was in medical school. Eventually, Michael was born. James' practice took off. We bought a house in Ballsbridge. We had a perfect life. I felt complete.

"Now it's all blown apart. James has a new younger wife, and Michael can't say more than three words to me at a time." She finished her wine and smiled at me. "But oh, did he pay!"

I burst out laughing at that last comment. Sorcha joined me. Michael returned and without a word settled down in his mother's old seat, his attention still fixated on his phone. Sorcha looked at him, the love in her eyes radiating out at him.

If only he could see it, I thought.

"We need another drink," Sorcha said abruptly. "Waiter, waiter...yes, please come here." She gestured toward him. "We need another round. I'm having a Chardonnay and...and?" She fumbled for my name.

"Nancy." I looked at the waiter and said, "I'll have a Guinness."

"Okay, enough about me. Now tell me about the second woman. I suspect she's a bit more complicated."

Yes, she was. Quickly, I gave her the background information about Brynn. Then I paused. I couldn't quite articulate it yet, but something was waking up inside me. A realization was starting to bloom but hadn't come to the surface. It was lurking underneath my subconscious, teasing me.

"She sounds lovely." Sorcha paused and then looked directly at me. "I hope you don't mind me saying this, but I think if she wanted to be with you, she would have made more of an effort."

It finally became clear.

"I think I really wanted Brynn to be Beth. I didn't know it at the time. But now I finally understand. I was in love with a ghost, and I wanted her to be that ghost. The more she slipped away, the harder I held on. I couldn't accept losing again.

"What I didn't realize, honestly until just now, was that what I feared losing was already gone. But Brynn was not gone, and I hung onto false hope that somehow it would all work out. It's why I lied to her and said I could be satisfied with just being friends. But I couldn't. I lied to her and I lied to myself."

Sorcha smiled. "So now that you know this, what are you going to do about it?"

"I don't know. I really don't know. Brynn won't talk to me, so I can't explain myself or make amends. I guess I'll have to learn to live with it. An unrequited love, an absolution that won't be given."

"Are you talking about her or yourself?" Sorcha asked, matter-of-factly. "I think you need to find it for yourself. It's not up to her to give that to you."

The directness of her words stung, but she was right. It wasn't up to anyone other than me to figure out how to deal with this.

LOST SOULS

I stopped, stood up, and yawned. It was getting late, but I was so close to the end. I wanted to finish. I gazed over at Jen who looked deep in thought. Or maybe she was asleep. I peered closer to see which it was.

"I'm still awake," Jen said in answer to my unasked question. She looked directly at me, her eyes thoughtful. "So, have you? Have you dealt with it?"

I stopped stretching and looked up at the night sky. "Not really. When I got back here, I called Brynn, but she wouldn't take my call. I left a message but no response. And that's it."

I paused. I continued to stare up at the stars, one flickered and then disappeared. "I've thought about this a lot. No easy answers come to me. But I think what saddens me the most is knowing I will not talk to her again. We won't have those wonderful conversations like we used to. I miss her laugh. I miss her perspective on issues we discussed. I miss her zest for life. I miss…I miss her."

I looked at Jen. "I have accepted my actions. My stupid, selfish behavior. I mean, really, showing up drunk…how pathetic. All along I should have been more honest about my feelings, instead of pretending that I was fine with us only being friends. But I wasn't and I wasn't brave enough to tell her. I was a coward. I was afraid to lose her. I desperately wanted her in my life and to be part of hers. Unrealistically thinking that someday she would feel the same way toward me.

"I think back now, and I see how it ate away at me. I lost myself. Or more accurately, I destroyed myself by not facing up to the truth and moving on. I lived a life of denial, waiting and wanting her. I think now that part of me wanted to end it, to move on. To stop living like a thief in the shadows waiting for an opportunity. I now wonder if this wasn't part of the reason I got so shitfaced. Did something completely outrageous, so disrespectful that she would reject me, even as a friend.

"She should move on. Stop wasting her time with a fool like me. In fact, I'm happy for her. I'm glad she moved on."

Jen simply stared at me.

I looked away. Still now, after all this time, my emotions threatened to choke me up. I sat back down, defeated.

"I'm lying. No, I'm not glad she moved on. I'm miserable. I wish I could tell you that when I came back, we talked and we made peace. That I told her everything I just said to you. But it didn't happen. And it is what it is. This is a regret that I will live with. But I will live. I will move forward and take this lesson with me. I will let it strengthen me. What *has* changed is that I now know I will never treat someone so disrespectfully again. I truly wronged her, and I will always regret that."

"It's a soul hurt," Jen said.

"A what?"

"A soul hurt. It's when you wrong someone or are wronged by someone on a soul level. It's a deep hurt. Like a sword has been plunged into you. No superficial words can remove it. No meaningless gestures can heal the wound. Only the truth can. Only genuine remorse for the wrong can pull the sword out."

"I get it. I truly get it. This is exactly how I feel. When I think about what I did, I feel like a lost soul. I don't think I would have understood this before my journey. I don't think I would have had the strength to accept this about myself."

"So now that you have come to admit all this, can you pull that sword out of yourself?" Jen asked.

I gave a weak smile. "I'll try."

Now it was Jen's turn to yawn and stretch. "How much more of this story is there?"

"Not much, I'm almost done. I know it's getting late, but just give me a few more minutes and I'll wrap this up."

"Great. I'm really interested, just getting tired," she said.

"Before I continue on with the next day, I'm going to tell you about the rest of that night and another lost soul I met."

This piqued Jen's attention. She sat up, ready to hear this next part of the story.

"Sorcha and I talked some more, mostly about her situation, and then we said our goodbyes. I thought about going to the other pub Moira mentioned, but I was exhausted. So, I called it a night.

"I got back to my room, probably around ten p.m., and quickly went to sleep. It was sometime in the middle of the night when I felt something on my legs. It was a kneading sensation. I was someplace between being asleep and awake. I tried to wake up fully, but I couldn't. I couldn't move either. Now I unmistakably felt a kneading pressure on my legs. Like a cat trying to find a place to lay down. Problem was there wasn't a cat in the room. At least not one alive.

"I was frozen, unable to speak or move. Fear gripped at me as I lay prone at the mercy of this paranormal visitor. It's a strange and disconcerting feeling to be unable to move. Now I was fully awake. I was screaming in my head, but nothing came out of my mouth. I strained to move my legs, but they were dead to my commands. I just lay there helpless, and all the while this thing was moving all over my legs and stomach."

"Oh my God!" Jen broke in, "I'd be terrified!"

"I wasn't terrified, but I was definitely scared. It had control of me physically. I think that's what bothered me the most. I kept trying to rationalize it. I tried to convince myself that I was still asleep, and this was just a dream. Only it wasn't, and I wasn't asleep. I began to panic—would this ever end? It seemed to be going on for a very long time.

"Just when I thought I couldn't take it anymore, I felt a rush of energy move up over my chest, stop, flutter like a caress against my right cheek, and then leave.

"And just like that," I snapped my fingers, "I was released. A bolt of electricity flew through me, and I leapt out of bed and turned on the light. I don't know why, but somehow having the light on made it all seem safe. Completely irrational, when you think about it."

Jen burst out laughing. "Yes, but I would have done the same. Actually, I would have run out the door screaming."

"Ha-ha, I would have too, but I was hyperventilating too much. I just stood there looking around at what appeared to be a normal bedroom. I picked up my phone off the nightstand and saw that it was two a.m.

"I didn't know what to do. It was too early to stay up, but I was afraid to go back to bed. I decided to lay back into bed and got on my phone. I distracted myself by going through my social media. Eventually, the adrenaline came down and I began to feel sleepy.

"I looked at the time. It was almost three a.m. If I was going to be able to do anything tomorrow, I needed to go back to sleep. I looked around the room, it all seemed normal. I sighed and turned out the light.

"As I lay on my pillow, I started to giggle and thought how absurd I was going to seem when I told people about my cat ghost."

DAY SEVEN

SÍ AN BHRÚ

I woke up to a bright sunny morning. The events of the night were still fresh as I lay in the bed and looked out the window to the garden. It was early, but I felt an urgency to get up. I was going to Newgrange today. I didn't know why, but the thought would not leave me. I felt compelled to go.

I got up and went to the shower. As the warm water cascaded over me, I thought again of my paranormal visitor. I could still feel its kneading on my legs, my immobility, and the flutter of energy as it moved up my body, caressed my cheek, and left.

I wrestled with whether I should mention any of it to my host. She might be okay and even joke about it. Maybe it was a common occurrence in this room. It was a very old house, and it wouldn't be unheard of for such a house to have some lingering residents. But what if she didn't know about it or, worse, thought I just trying to make trouble? That was the last thing I wanted.

I was still debating with myself when I entered the breakfast room. I took a seat at a small table, and Katherine entered the room.

"Ah, I see you are an early riser. Must be from your years as a horsewoman," she joked. "I hope you slept alright? Now, do you want coffee or tea?"

"Coffee please." I didn't know how to answer. Should I tell her? I was the only guest with her at the moment. If I was going to say anything, now was the time. "Actually, I wanted to ask you…"

I stopped abruptly as a couple entered the room.

"Be right with you," Katherine cheerfully called over to them. "Now, what did you want to ask me?"

I stammered. "Oh…I just…I just…wanted to…well, it can wait. Why don't you go over and help them?"

Smiling, Katherine turned and went over to the other couple. I took a deep breath. I knew now that I wasn't going to bring up whether she knew she had a cat ghost. A few moments later, she returned with my coffee.

"Now, what is it you wanted to ask me?" she said as she filled my cup from the coffee pot.

"Oh yes, well, I wanted to get your opinion. I'm thinking of going up to Newgrange today. Is that feasible?"

I knew full well I was going to Newgrange. I just had to think of something to ask her, and this was the only thing I could think of.

"Oh sure, it's a bit of a hike, but yes, very feasible if you leave early. But take the M9."

The breakfast room started to fill up with other guests. I ate my breakfast and then prepared to leave. After I got my bags in the car, I came back to pay for the room.

"Thank you again for letting me stay for the night."

"Oh, my pleasure. Now be careful, but I hope you have a wonderful time. I wish I was brave enough to go out on my own. Newgrange is very interesting, you'll be glad you went."

"Thanks! Next time I'm definitely spending more time here," I said.

With that, she turned and went back to the kitchen. I looked at her and smiled. Yes, I was definitely coming back. I didn't even scratch the surface of all the wonderful places and things to do here. I felt like this was a teaser for my next adventure.

Before I stepped into the car, I looked around. I loved it here in Ireland. This was my last day, and already I was longing to return. I sighed and got in the car. Soon I made my way to the motorway and started my trek up north.

<hr />

For the first time on this trip, my journey was uneventful. The GPS worked perfectly, and I made it to the Brú na Bóinne complex with no detours or side diversions. When I pulled into the parking area, it was full of cars. Buses were pulling in and out. Everywhere there were people walking. I began to doubt why I felt compelled to come here. This whole trip I'd been avoiding crowds like this. Now on the last day of this magical journey, I found myself at a tourist trap.

Without question, I had followed the force to this place. Was I delusional? What made me think this was going to be something special for me on my journey? Was I spoiled after having so many unique and personal experiences? So many questions. I felt tested. I had no idea what the correct answers were or what feelings I should be having. Should it be gratitude? Humility? Maybe I was here because of my hubris?

"Fuck it," I said. "Britt, you want to see this, so go see it. Don't make it any more complicated than that."

With that, I got out of the car and made my way over to the main entrance. It seemed a bit disorganized. There were what looked like temporary trailers which had windows where people were queuing up to get tickets. I looked across from the trailers and saw a long, covered waiting area filled with people.

It all seemed a bit dumpy, especially for a designated World Heritage site by UNESCO. I walked up to the trailer and waited for my turn in line. I didn't see any indication of how much it was going to cost, which I thought was weird. But unless it was astronomical, I was going to do it. All I saw was a board that listed the times for tours. I also noticed there were times for tours of just Newgrange or for both Newgrange and Knowth.

Slowly I made my way into the line, and eventually it was my turn. The lady working the ticket booth was very matter of fact.

"What tour are you doing?"

"I'm not sure. How long do the tours take? Actually, how much do they cost?"

"Nothing. It's free."

"Free?"

She let out a sigh which told me that she had already heard that reaction at least four hundred times today alone. "Yes. Our visitor center is being redone. So, the only services we are offering now are visits to the sites."

"Oh wow! Well, great. How long does the Knowth and Newgrange tour take?"

"It runs about three hours."

I knew that was going to be too long, given the time of day. I still had to get back to Dublin, return the car, and check in to my hotel. Also, I felt a strong urge for me to just go to Newgrange. It was almost insistent.

"I think I'll just do the Newgrange tour," I said.

Without a word, she slipped me a piece of paper with a time on it. "That's your ticket to board the bus. Just go over to the waiting area and get in line."

I took the ticket and looked over at the mass of humanity standing in line under the long wooden covering. Resigned, I made my way over and took a place in line. Luckily the line moved fairly quickly, and soon I was walking with my allotted group toward the area where the buses were located.

We walked down a wooden boardwalk through dense vegetation. The path went over the River Boyne, and I slowed down and looked at the beauty all around me. People rushed past, eager to get to the buses, oblivious to the incredible scenery around them. Unlike the woman I was seven days ago in the San Francisco airport, rushing to keep up with total strangers, now I could care less. I was no longer that woman. I fell behind as the crowd rushed past.

This was Ireland in her gorgeous splendor, and I had no desire to rush past her. The river was wide and deep. Trees grew thick along the riverbank, broken up by intrusions of meadows saturated by the overflowing river water. Shrubs with bright red berries and tall grasses mixed in between the trees and meadows. Birds were singing their songs.

The path made its way through this Eden until it ended at an area where the buses pulled in to be loaded. As I waited to board one, I found that I was surrounded by what seemed to be loud, obnoxious Americans and intense Germans. I hated to admit it, but one could spot an American tourist blindfolded. That boisterous Southern drawl permeated everything.

I stayed silent and kept to myself. The driver came on and explained how everything worked. I only sort of paid attention, a disassociation seemed to be taking hold of me. This was starting to feel more like a pilgrimage. I was going to a tomb. A sacred site. An ancient site. I needed to give it the reverence it deserved.

I took a seat, and as the bus started to pull out, I reflected on the fact that this was my last day in Ireland. Tomorrow I headed back to the United States. Back to my other reality. I didn't want it to end. I wanted to stay in this state. Neither forward nor backward; just present. I had journeyed a lifetime, maybe several, while here.

The bus drove along a country lane past farms, until eventually, it pulled up to the unloading area. People pushed their way off and rushed to the gatehouse. Again, I followed everyone, and by the time I got there, a park official was out front instructing us to wait until our guide came to collect us and take us up to the site.

But what a tease it was to wait. Up on a hill, the monument towered over everything. Its white rock sides contrasted against the green grass of its dome and the surrounding landscape. Needless to say, it was impressive to look at. The crowd anxiously waited for the guide. I watched as some paced about and others could be heard grumbling about having to wait. To them, this was just another thing to check off their sightseeing list.

I sensed someone next to me and turned my head to see a diminutive dark-haired woman stride past with a confidence that belied her small stature. She moved up in front of the crowd. With a no-nonsense stance, she turned and faced the group. People stopped pacing. Silence ensued. She had effortlessly taken command.

"Hello and welcome to the World Heritage site of Newgrange. I am Siobhan, and I will be your guide today. Due to the age and complexities of the architecture, only small groups are allowed into the structure. Follow me as we walk up to the main entrance area, and I will explain the significance of the standing stones and why the ancient people chose this location for the building of this passage tomb."

Without waiting for any comments or questions, she abruptly turned and started up the path toward the monument. Quickly, everyone fell into line and followed her up the hill. It was a steep incline, and the group began to spread out as people made their way up. Once we all gathered again in front of the standing stones where Siobhan was waiting, she began explaining why the area was important to the ancient people who lived here and why they chose this particular site for the passage tomb.

"Now, that completes what I have to tell you so far. You have fifteen minutes until our group will be called to enter the main tomb. Please feel free to explore the outside of the monument, but make sure you are back here in time."

The group broke apart. Some people took off to walk around the circumference, others were pelting the guide with questions. I walked away to look at the view of the river valley below. Just like the cathedrals I had seen on this trip, this place was situated prominently so it could be admired by its faithful.

Religion is a tricky subject for me. I struggle with dogma but embrace the mystery. I love rituals, but rebel against absolutes. I don't believe any one gender, race, or religion has the absolute truth. It's bigger than that for me. I love the sanctuaries of the cathedral and the forest equally.

I reflected that this trip had been about me finding my faith again. Faith in myself. Faith in others. Faith in the divine. I closed my eyes and felt the warmth of the sun on my face. Here it was so easy to embrace it all. Here I had walked on both sides of the veil. *How will I keep this part of me alive when I leave?*

I opened my eyes and looked at the valley below. *I wish I could go back in time. I wish I could be part of these people. I wish I had their convictions of faith. I wish I had made better choices.*

I bowed my head and fought back tears. Then, like a comforting hand, I felt the force and heard its voice.

> *I know of the world you live in.*
> *Science is your religion,*
> *skepticism your God*
> *Mysticism is sacrificed on the altar of rationality.*
>
> *But look, this place is born of both,*
> *science and mysticism.*
> *One does not exist without the other.*
> *This your ancestors understood.*
>
> *You have lost so much separating the two.*
> *Now you reduce yourselves to particles and give them names,*
> *categories,*
> *designations.*
>
> *But in the process, you lost your greatness,*
> *your humanity,*
> *your soul.*
>
> *You feel lost and uncertain,*
> *questioning all you hold dear*
> *Afraid one wrong answer will lead to ruin*
> *But nothing could be further from the truth.*

You are supposed to fail,
to question,
to despair.

An untested metal shatters with the first strike
It takes many hits to temper the blade.
Just so, you are like metal
and your life has been the hammer.

Take heart, my daughter, you are at Sí an Bhrú
Walk in and take the gift it is meant to give.

This is your birthright.

With my head still bowed, I choked back a sob. But it wasn't a cry of anguish. It was an overwhelming sense of gratitude. It was not a mistake to come here. An answer waited for me.

Before I could process any more, I saw people in my group starting to head toward the opening. I followed, anxious. Soon I would see what awaited. As I walked, I looked up to the opening where our guide stood waiting. Our eyes locked with intensity. Silently, I walked up and queued up with the rest. She continued to stare and then shifted to her task at hand.

"Alright. Very good. You all made it back. Now a few details before we enter. No photography is allowed. Also, mute your phones. The passage into the chamber gets narrow. So, take off all backpacks. If you are claustrophobic, you will probably want to be toward the back. Once inside, we will be quite packed."

A group exited as she made her speech. To enter, we had to ascend a wooden staircase that then dropped down toward the passageway. Knowing I suffered from claustrophobia, I hung back so that I could enter toward the last of the group. I was glad I did. Once you passed through the opening, the path narrowed considerably.

People bumped into each other the farther we progressed and the darker it became. I was wondering how much further we had to go and how much more closed-in it would get before I couldn't take it anymore. I knew I had to get in. I was meant to be here. I hung onto that thought as I squeezed through the passageway.

Just as I thought I couldn't go anymore, it opened up, and we stepped into the inner chamber. The space was very dark, with only a few accent lights. I found a place against one of the walls.

Everything was silent.

Siobhan started to tell the history of the tomb. She described its architecture, its rediscovery, the human remains, and at last, she addressed its most famous aspect. The winter solstice. This was the reason most people came. The incredible phenomenon of the entry of light into the inner chamber for over five thousand years on the winter solstice.

To dramatize the event, all lights were shut off. The tomb was plunged into a darkness I had never felt before. The fact that we were in a tomb was forced upon us. You could not see your own hand if you held it before your eyes.

The temperature felt colder.

The air was heavy.

Everything was silent.

I looked back from where we entered. Barely visible was a cool blue glow from the entryway. It seemed so far away. I was in the void. I felt the grip of death on me. I felt fear. Then dimly, a light came, and as it grew stronger, it traveled the pathway until it reached the chamber. The comfort, hope, and miracle of light filled the space. Fear subsided with the shaft of light. I looked at the passageway. Then I knew. I knew the gift.

The ancients understood. Oh, this beautiful blend of science and mysticism. This was not a tomb, this was a womb. This is why I had to come. This was my rebirth. This was my reincarnation.

A flash of light exploded to my left. I looked and saw a woman with her phone held up in her hand. The intrusion felt like a violation. Before anyone could react, I heard Siobhan.

"Put that down!"

All I could see of Siobhan was a red glare from where her eyes should be. In what seemed an instant, Siobhan was next to the woman.

"Give that to me!" she said insistently.

Overwhelmed by the ferocity of Siobhan's demand, the woman meekly handed over her phone. Siobhan took it, and I saw her delete the photo.

"You were told no photos!"

Siobhan was fearsome in her rage. The woman said something in German that sounded like it was an apology. I took a quick intake of breath as I realized that Siobhan was more than what she presented. Sensing my realization, she shot me a direct look. I knew instantly that I was not to say anything.

Having dealt with the situation, Siobhan made a few closing remarks and directed everyone to leave so that the next group could come in. I lingered as the group began to make its way back down the passageway.

When there were only a few people left, I made my way over to her. She was standing in the center of the chamber. A fierce protector of this realm. As I approached, her eyes softened, and she smiled.

The veil is thin here, I thought.

"I want to talk to you," I said.

She smiled and nodded in acceptance of my request. I could tell she was expecting me.

"As we were standing in here, I was overcome with the realization that this place is more than a tomb. I feel like it is a womb. That…that it's about rebirth…um, I mean reincarnation. Am I making any sense?"

I looked into the blackness of her eyes and saw the glow of flames in them.

"Yes, you are making sense. Just look at the basins that held the deceased's remains; they are shaped like birthing basins. Now look again at the passageway; it is the birthing canal," she said. Then softly, she added. "There is so much more here than what you can see."

I turned and looked at the passageway, but now instead of narrow and forbidding, it looked wide open and inviting. I turned back to her but couldn't speak. I felt like I would burst apart, overcome by the flow of love filling me up. I couldn't even begin to understand, much less express my joy and gratitude.

Siobhan said nothing. No words were needed. We understood each other perfectly. Not only was she the custodian and protector of this sacred place, she was also the gift bearer. She was here to help me; she was my guide. With a trust I had never felt before, I closed my eyes and accepted my death.

I accepted the death of my fear, failures, doubts, and shortcomings. I accepted the death of my sorrows, heartbreaks, and desolation. My sadness, hatred, and self-loathing were all allowed to die. I accepted the death of all that I had done and been, as well as all that had been done to me.

I felt her hand on my arm, and I opened my eyes.

"It's time to go," she whispered.

I nodded and walked ahead of her through the passageway. As I neared the exit, I blinked from the brightness of the sunlight. I felt a lightness in my step and, for a moment, visualized myself in flight in the bright blue sky, looking down at the grassy hillside and the Boyne River.

As I stepped out, I saw the impatient stares of the next guide and the people waiting to get in. Unfazed, I smiled at them and ascended the other set of steps out of the opening. Once I descended onto the ground on the other side, I turned back to say something to Siobhan. But she was not there. I looked back at the opening, but she wasn't there either. I looked all around the area, but she was nowhere to be found.

Alone, I stood on the gravel outside the opening. I stared at the green fields and the river down below me. I saw a bus pull into the loading area and recognized members of my group boarding it. Nonchalantly, I watched them board the bus. I was no longer part of the group but didn't care.

The sun, unrestricted from the rain clouds that had blocked her for most of the week, blazed down. I closed my eyes and bent my neck back to feel its heat on my face. A slight breeze swept over my face and softly tossed the loose ends of my hair that had escaped my ponytail.

As I stood on the grave of my ancestors, their strength and spirit flowed within me. They were now a part of me as I was of them. With gratitude and humility, I accepted my transformation.

Without our failures, loves, losses, and triumphs, there would be no growth. No enlightenment. There would be no hammer to temper our steel. It wasn't as if I would never experience heartache or loss again. That wouldn't be real, and it wouldn't be good. What had changed was my ability to deal with it all.

One thing I was certain of was this: I would once again laugh so hard I'd pee my pants, grieve until it felt like my heart would burst, sit alone in the desolation of loneliness, and happily curl up in the companionship of a loving embrace.

This time when I heard the voice, I felt a bit sad. I knew our time was ending.

It's time for you to go, my child,
back to your family and friends.

No longer are you lost
that which was broken has mended.

Go forth bravely and with kindness

And know you are never alone.

I am always within you.

I am always your home.

ACKNOWLEDGMENTS

This work has been a journey that has had many helping hands and hearts along the way. First, I would like to thank Thea Rademacher of Flint Hills Publishing for having faith in me and this story. To my editor, Paul Fredrickson who understood what I was trying to say and shared in my vision for this book. To Jennifer Anderson, who saw the writer in me and helped me to find my voice. I am also indebted to my parents, who gave me the freedom to be myself even when they didn't understand or agree. To my siblings, for their love and support and excruciating teasing, especially when things were tough. I also want to thank my friends who have stood by me through thick and thin; you know who you are. Lastly, I want to thank that which has no name but resides within all living beings. Thank you for waking me up, I will never be the same.

ABOUT THE AUTHOR

Nancy M. Britt grew up in the mountains and deserts of the Southwestern United States, the daughter of an exploration geologist.

As a young adult in the 1980s, she came out as a lesbian and witnessed first-hand the devastation of the AIDs epidemic. She proudly participated in marches against inequality and was a part of the emerging lesbian presence in American society. Graduating from the University of Denver College of Law, she worked as a trial attorney for many years until taking a position as a Legal Editor with LexisNexis.

Today she is the owner of a successful training and coaching equestrian business, Kildare Farms, operating out of Tucson, Arizona.

www.nancymbritt.com